THE QUEEN AND I:

The Play with Songs

Sue Townsend

songs by Ian Dury and Mickey Gallagher

**The Royal Court Writers series published by
Methuen Drama in association with
the Royal Court Theatre**

Royal Court Writers series

The Queen and I: The Play with Songs was first published in Great Britain in the Royal Court Writers series in 1994 by
Methuen Drama
an imprint of Reed Consumer Books Ltd
Michelin House, 81 Fulham Road, London SW3 6RB
and Auckland, Melbourne, Singapore and Toronto
in association with the Royal Court Theatre
Sloane Square, London SW1N 8AS

The Queen and I: The Play copyright © 1994 by Sue Townsend
Songs copyright © 1994 Ian Dury and Mickey Gallagher
The author has asserted her moral rights

ISBN 0–413–68970–0

A CIP catalogue record for this book
is available from the British Library

Typeset by Wilmaset Ltd, Birkenhead, Wirral
Printed and bound in Great Britain by
Cox & Wyman Ltd, Cardiff Road, Reading, Berkshire

The Haymarket Theatre, Leicester, Out of Joint and the Royal Court Theatre present

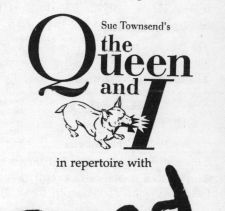

Sue Townsend's

the Queen and I

in repertoire with

Road

by Jim Cartwright

The Queen and I
First performed at the Haymarket Theatre, Leicester 23rd March 1994
First performed at the Royal Court Theatre 7th June 1994

Road
First performed at the Royal Court Theatre Upstairs 22nd March 1986
First performance of this production at the Theatre Royal, Bath 22nd April 1994
First performance of this production at the Royal Court Theatre 9th June 1994

The Royal Court Theatre is financially assisted by the Royal Borough of Kensington and Chelsea.
Recipient of a grant from the Theatre Restoration Fund & from the Foundation for Sport & the Arts
The Royal Court's Play Development Programme is funded by the Audrey Skirball-Kenis Theatre
Registered Charity number 231242

HAYMARKET THEATRE LEICESTER

The Haymarket Theatre, Leicester

Out of Joint

OUT OF JOINT

Chief Executive	**John Blackmore**
Artistic Director	**Paul Kerryson**
Administrator	**Tana Wolf**
Head of Marketing	**Tracey Waters**
Production Manager	**Steve Green**
Education Administrator	**Ellen Bianchini**
Press Enquiries	**Paul Willerton**

The Haymarket Theatre acknowledges financial support fron East Midlands Arts, Leicester City Council and Leicestershire County Council. Registered Charity number 230708

Director	**Max Stafford-Clark**
Producer	**Sonia Friedman**
Production Manager	**Iain Gillie**
Sound Engineer	**Simon Baker**
Marketing	**Guy Chapman**
Press	**Cameron Duncan**
Assistant to the Director	**Alexandra Roberts**
Production Assistant	**Tom Hillier**

Out of Joint is a new touring theatre company established by Max Stafford-Clark and Sonia Friedman. The company will perform a new play alongside a classic; the two plays will then be toured in repertoire nationwide. Registered Charity number 1033059. Out of Joint would particularly like to thank the following, The John S Cohen Foundation, The Olivier Foundation, The Paul Hamlyn Foundation, Stephen Evans and Karl Sydow and Arts Council Touring

THE ENGLISH STAGE COMPANY AT THE ROYAL COURT THEATRE

The English Stage Company was formed to bring serious writing back to the stage. The Court's first Artistic Director, George Devine, wanted to create a vital and popular theatre. In order to promote this, he encouraged new writing that explored subjects drawn from contemporary life as well as pursuing European plays and forgotten classics. When John Osborne's **Look Back in Anger** was first produced in 1956, and revived in '57, it forced British Theatre into the modern age. At the same time Brecht, Giraudoux, Ionesco and Sartre were also part of the repertoire.

The ambition to discover new work which was challenging, innovative and also of the highest quality became the fulcrum of the Company's course of action. Early Court writers included Arnold Wesker, John Arden, David Storey, Ann Jellicoe, N F Simpson and Edward Bond. They were followed by a generation of writers led by David Hare and Howard Brenton, and in more recent years, celebrated house writers have included Caryl Churchill, Timberlake Wertenbaker, Robert Holman and Jim Cartwright. Many of their plays are now regarded as modern classics.

In line with the policy of nurturing new writing, the Theatre Upstairs has mainly been seen as a place for exploration and experiment, where writers learn and develop their skills prior to the demands of the main stage auditorium. Anne Devlin, Andrea Dunbar, Sarah Daniels, Jim Cartwright, Clare McIntyre, Winsome Pinnnock, and more recently Martin Crimp have, or will in the future, benefit from this process. The Theatre Upstairs proved its value as a focal point for new work with the production of the Chilean writer Ariel Dorfman's **Death and the Maiden**. More recently talented young writers as diverse as Jonathan Harvey, Adam Pernak, Phyllis Nagy (in association with the Liverpool Playhouse) and Gregory Motton (in association with the Royal National Theatre Studio) have been shown to great advantage in this space.

1991, 1992, and 1993 have been record-breaking years at the box-office with capacity houses for productions of **Top Girls**, **Three Birds Alighting on a Field**, **Faith Healer**, **Death and the Maiden**, **Six Degrees of Separation**, **King Lear**, **Oleanna** and **The Kitchen**. **Death and the Maiden** and **Six Degrees of Separation** won the Olivier Award for Best Play in 1992 and 1993 respectively. **Three Birds Alighting on a Field** was awarded Best West End Play by the Writer's Guild of Great Britain, and recently enjoyed a successful revival at New York's Manhattan Theatre Club.

After nearly four decades, the Royal Court Theatre is still a major focus in the country for the production of new work. Scores of plays first seen in Sloane Square are now part of the National and International dramatic repertoire.

Photo: Ivan Kyncl

Arnold Wesker's **The Kitchen**

While working on *THE QUEEN AND I* and *ROAD*, the company kept a scrapbook...

200 RAIDS BY TEARAWAY, 14

A boy of 14 is responsible for 200 store burglaries which have cost traders in just one street £200,000. He and his gang are behind 97 per cent of a town's shop break-ins say police. The 80 shops preyed on by the artful dodger include Marks and Spencer, Currys, Dixons, Burtons and Mothercare. The gang even leave behind gloating calling cards saying "In case of emergency dial 999".

The Sun July 1993

DESPAIR ON THE BREADLINE

Across the Tyne the lights of the Metro Centre twinkle and taunt. The country's biggest out-of-town shopping centre stands as Mammon to many in Newcastle's impoverished West End - a daily reminder of what they cannot have or even aspire to.

Instead, there are queues for reject bread outside Gregg's Seconds Bakery, at jumble sales and at the job centre. In common with families on other estates fringing the northern banks of the Tyne, many in north Benwell are suffering the effects of grinding poverty.

There is malnutrition, high infant mortality, poor physical and mental health. On two of the estates, Save the Children, a charity more usually associated with Third-World poverty, is starting up healthy communitites projects.

On Benwell the rows of Victorian back-to-backs are nightly disintegrating into a ghetto. Down darkened streets are the hulks of burnt out homes and shops. Others stand boarded up and vandalised as the past two years have seen an exodus of those able to flee what has become, for many, a crime-ridden slum. A glimpse of light behind a boarded-up window suggests someone in refuge.

Those left behind feel abandoned as their streets are littered with uncollected rubbish, broken glass and the debris of previous nights of mischief; burnt tyres, a wrecked car.

The Independent August 1993

THE DRUGS EXPLOSION

Drug abuse is becoming an every day experience for millions of Britain's children thanks to dealing in playgrounds.

That is the conclusion of drug experts and is supported by inquiries by The Independent, which discovered evidence of a new narcotics craze among children as young as 10 who are buying sleeping tablets for as little as 50p each. There is also evidence of widespread dealing and use of illegal substances in schools. In one London comprehensive in a middle-class area a gang of 14 and 15-year-olds sell cannabis in the playground.

An unpublished study funded by the Department of Health, which looked at schools in northern England, reveals drug abuse by children aged from 13 to 18 is commonplace.

The Independent August 1993

TEENAGE TRADEGY

It's open season on teenage mothers again. In July Welsh Secretary John Redwood announced his shock at discovering that on some Cardiff housing estates young women have babies "with no apparent intention of even trying marriage or a stable relationship with the father of the child". Days later, Health Minister Tom Sackville chose the anniversary of the publication of the Health of the Nation report to complain that the provision of council housing and welfare benefits had encouraged teenage mothers.

If single-motherhood appears attractive to young working class women it is because they have no prospect of doing anything more significant with their lives. Ask any 13-year old girl what she wants to be when she's 17 and you won't find one that aspires to being a teenage mother. She wants a job, a wage, a nice boyfriend, friends and a hectic social life. Motherhood only becomes attractive when it's compared to living out your unemployed days in your mum's flat with no income to call your own.

Living Marxism August 1993

TYNE SIDES

The criminologist who warned last week of a time when cities might be walled so social "undesirables" could be excluded from more affluent "fortress" areas would doubtless have interesting views on Newcastle upon Tyne.

Two years ago this week, this city was subjected to a sort of social pincer attack when criminal or wayward standard bearers for the poor and the unemployed declared war on the seeming hopelessness of their situation. Hundreds of thousands of pounds worth of damage was caused in a few hours and by a relatively small number of people. These riots, according to Beatrix Campbell who now lives in Newcastle, were an explosion waiting to happen. But "they did not represent the people's collective will, they represented its defeat."

The Guardian September 1993

CHILD POVERTY BLAMED ON WELFARE CUTS

Britain has slipped in world league tables of children's health and welfare because of the Government's cutbacks in the welfare state, Unicef, the United Nations children's charity, said.

The Guardian October 1993

A SINGULAR VIEW OF SINGLE PARENTS

Sandra Gossey, chair of the estate residents' association, well remembers the day she welcomed the minister to St. Mellons. The Cabinet's latest recruit, only just appointed Secretary of State for Wales, shocked guests by asking bluntly what the churches were doing about teenage pregnancies. Eyebrows were raised.

He then asked his flabbergasted guests: "Does anyone make contact with the young people who father these children? They must be rather odd. Most fathers quite like being involved with children."

But worse was to come for St Mellons. Two days later, in a celebrated speech to party faithful which first raised the spectre of benefit cuts for lone mothers, Redwood called for tough action to discourage the growing trend of single-parent families: as he put it, "if someone is old enough to father a child, he should be old enough to bring it up."

To hammer home this theme, the minister spoke of a recent visit to an unnamed council estate where "over half" the houses were occupied by single parents. "What a nerve," thought Sandra, a married nurse who has lived on St Mellons for five years. "He's got the figures wrong."

The Guardian November 1993

ROLLER-COASTER RIDE TO DESPAIR

Haunted. That's the best word I can use to describe her. Nervous and haunted, labouring behind a pushchair up the hill, as if some ghost was on her trail. When I spoke to her in a cafe she was so startled she almost jumped. I only said "I've seen you up Housing Benefit Hill, haven't I?" After that we'd say hello and whatever; the usual politenesses. I met her in another cafe one day, and the person I was chatting to recognised her.

"Didn't we go to school together? It's Tamsin, isn't it? What have you been doing with yourself?"

"Nothing. I just made a stupid mistake and got married, that's all," she said, her normally timid voice tinged with an unexpected bitterness.

The Guardian Weekend February 1994

ABUSE BY CHILDREN AT RECORD LEVEL

Record numbers of children and young people are taking drugs in Britain, with an increasing range of illegal substances on offer.

There is also growing evidence that the age at which the young start to experiment has dropped in the last few years from 16 to about 14, though the bulk of drug education is still aimed at older children. Drug workers are also finding a significant number of children aged 10 and 11 are abusing substances such as solvents. A child of seven was the youngest to have been counselled for drug abuse at a project in London.

The largest national survey of drug use among the young reveals that the number of users has doubled every two years. Another study in the north-west of England shows that about half have taken drugs by the age of 16.

Sarah is 13. She takes LSD and sniffs glue and aerosols - gas lighter fuel and air fresheners are her favourites. "It's nothing unusual, people do it all the time," she says.

Another girl of the same age who goes to school in a rural part of Cleveland recalls how she and her friends sat outside the police headquarters in her local town and smoked cannabis.

"We were walking down with the spliff [cigarette] in our hands with the police cars driving past. A policeman came past and he said 'Do you always smoke rollies?'. The police knew nowt about it. We were all crapping ourselves, but laughing as well."
The Independent March 1994

BOYS, 6, WRECK NEIGHBOURS HOUSE 'FOR FUN'

Two six-year-old boys who broke into a neighbour's home and caused thousands of pounds' damage in a wrecking spree told police: "We wanted to have some fun".

The boys spent an hour destroying property at the house after smashing through the glass front door while the owners were away from home, on an estate which is a mixture of private and council owned property.

Although the youngsters were detained they will not be charged with burglary or criminal damage because they are under 10, the age of criminal responsibility. The mothers of both boys have asked for help from Hampshire social services, who received a report on the break-in from police.
The Times March 1994

LOCKING KIDS UP

Simon Hill has always been tall for his age. At 14 he stands at six feet in his Nike Air Jordans. His chubby face is wiped of expression; his dark hair is combed into a stiff side parting; he stares straight ahead of him with round, calm, dark brown eyes at the magistrate in Birmingham's Youth Courts.

Outside the court, the corridor wall bears scratched testimony to the children who have kicked along its chilly length down the years. Ajaz, Donna, Evo, Jon: every brick is signed by name or date or with the carver's offences - GBH (grevious bodily harm), ABH (actual bodily harm), TDA (taking and driving away). Simon's name is there, if you look hard enough, semi-hidden within the defiant scrapings of the never-say-die. F*** Da Police. Born To Be Wild. Or just - Bad.

In the glass-fronted waiting-room sit two lone women, a solicitor and a mother with her teenage boy. All are neatly dressed; the lad has his hair brushed uncomfortably forward. He's sitting having a cigarette with his solicitor. They talk urgently, with narrowed eyes and stabbing gestures, their feet on the seats in front in a parody of a mafiosi don and his consiglieri. The boy's mother, completely excluded, sits in the row behind.

Back in Court 2, the magistrate looks over her glasses and glares at Simon.

"Young Man," she is saying, "We have seen you before. Many people have suffered because of what you felt was an addiction. It is not our desire to deal with you so leniently, our hands are tied by the law of this country."

She speaks for a further three minutes. Then Simon Hill, 14 and two weeks, veteran of more than 200 crimes over the past 10 months, walks out of the court, turns quickly through a side exit, gets into a waiting car and drives home with his mum.
Observer (Life Magazine) April 1994

Director	**Max Stafford-Clark**
Designer	**Fotini Dimou**
Music and Lyrics (The Queen and I)	**Mickey Gallagher and Ian Dury**
Lighting Designer (The Queen and I)	**Rick Fisher**
Lighting Designer (Road)	**Johanna Town**
Sound Designer	**John A. Leonard**
Mask Designer (The Queen and I)	**Sally Cook**
Musical Director and Musician (The Queen and I)	**James Compton**
Movement (The Queen and I)	**Sue Lefton**
Fight Director (The Queen and I)	**Terry King**
Casting Director	**Lisa Makin**
Assistant Director	**Sally Cook**
Dialect and Voice Coach	**Joan Washington**
Company Stage Manager	**Jacqui McLeod-Kelly**
Deputy Stage Manager	**Justine Gallaccio**
Assistant Stage Manager	**Billy Haynes**
Costume Supervisor	**Iona Kenrick**
Production Wardrobe	**Sam Mealing**
Wardrobe Assistant	**Katy Griffith**
Production Carpenter	**Jerry Donaldson**
Production Electrician	**Ian Moulds**
Design Assistant	**Alex Hawkey**
Production Photographs	**John Haynes**
Leaflet and Poster Design	**The Loft**
Producer	**Sonia Friedman**

We would like to thank the following for their help with this production:

BBC Radio Leicester; The Royal National Theatre; The Manchester Tabacco Company; The National Canine Defence League; Kwik Silver Theatre Company; DHSS Newcastle Upon Tyne, Norcross, Leeds; Sainsburys plc; Louis Vuitton; The Sporting Life Ltd; Timex Corporation, UK Time Ltd; World Wide Fund for Nature; Maclaren; W.A.Ingrams (Zippo) Ltd; Ruddles Beer; Augustus Barnett; Sarah Beecham; Mid-Sat International; Hinkley for the Satellite Dish; Porth Decorative Products Ltd; Lucas Yuasa Batteries Birmingham; "Duchess" English Bone China; Motorola Ltd; Peeks of Bournemouth Christmas Tree Decorations; Multi-aerial Service Company Midlands; Marathon Motor Supplies Ltd; The Leicester Wholesale Fruit Market and

TOSHIBA

Wardrobe care by Persil and Comfort courtesy of Lever Brothers Ltd; watches by The Timex Corporation; refrigerators by Electrolux and Philips Major Appliances Ltd.; kettles for rehearsals by Morphy Richards; video for casting purposes by Hitachi; backstage coffee machine by West 9; furniture by Knoll International; freezer for backstage use supplied by Zanussi Ltd 'Now that's a good idea.'; Hair by Carole at Edmond's, 19 Beauchamp Place, SW3; closed circuit TV cameras and monitors by Mitsubishi UK Ltd; natural spring water from Wye Spring Water, 149 Sloane Street, London SW1, tel. 071-730 6977; overhead projector from W.H. Smith.

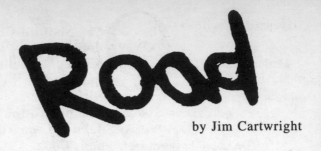

Road

by Jim Cartwright

**The performance lasts approximately 2 hours and 15 minutes.
There will be an interval of 15 minutes**

in repertoire with

Sue Townsend's
the **Queen** and **I**

CAST	in alphabetical order
Leanne Trish	**Amelia Bullmore**
The Queen	**Pam Ferris**
Queen Mother Crawfire Amanda Boniface	**Gillian Hanna**
Princess Margaret Violet Toby	**Carole Hayman**
Prince Philip D.I. Holyland Wilf Toby	**David Howey**
Princess Diana	**Doon Mackichan**
Fitzroy Mrs Toussaint	**Paul J. Medford**
Prince William Dorkin P.C. Ludlow Mrs Newman	**Pearce Quigley**
Prince Charles Spiggy	**Toby Salaman**

**The performance lasts approximately 2 hours and 40 minutes.
There will be an interval of 15 minutes**

BIOGRAPHIES

SUE TOWNSEND

Sue Townsend was born and still lives in Leicestershire.

Plays: ten performed plays.

Books include: The Secret Diary of Adrian Mole, Rebuilding Coventry, The Wilderness Years, The Queen and I, Mr Bevan's Dream.

TV scripts include: The Secret Diary of Adrian Mole, Bodies.

Films include: Rebuilding Coventry, Adios (current projects).

Radio includes: The Secret Diary, The Queen and I, The Wilderness Years, The Ashes, A Ladder in Her Stocking.

JIM CARTWRIGHT

Jim Cartwright was born and lives in Lancashire. His first play Road was performed at the Royal Court in 1986 then revived in 19897 and taken on a nationwide tour.

Plays include: Road (Samuel Beckett Award, Drama Magazine Award, joint winner of the George Devine award, Plays and Players award); Bed, Two (Manchester Evening News Best Play Award); The Rise and Fall of Little Voice (1992 Evening Standard Award for Best Comedy, 1993 Olivier Award for Best Comedy).

TV scripts include: Road (Golden Nymph Award); June; Wedded.

Films include: Vroom.

Radio includes: Baths.

AMELIA BULLMORE

Theatre includes: Major Barbara, Sweet Bird of Youth (Citizen's, Glasgow); Romeo and Juliet, A View from the Bridge (Royal Exchange, Manchester); All My Sons, How the Other Half Loves (Everyman, Cheltenham); Threepenny Opera (Birmingham Rep); Be Bop a Lula (Liverpool Playhouse); The Red Balloon (Contact, Manchester), Inadmissable Evidence (RNT).

TV includes: Coronation Street, Stuck on You, Cracker, Faith.

Radio includes: Villette, The Frightful Thing, Life with Lederer, The Leftover Heart.

Founder member of Red Stockings Theatre Company; member of Comedy Express.

JAMES COMPTON (musical director)

Formerly producing and writing for bands; now concentrates on theatre, television and radio as Music Director and performer.

Theatre includes: Yakety Yak (Half Moon, Astoria, international tour); Buddy Holly Live at Crewe (Young Vic tour); Beehive (Newcastle Playhouse); Good Rockin' Tonight (West End); Leader of the Pack, Fabulous Singlettes (Duke of York's); Lipstick Dreams (Shaw). Forever Plaid (Apollo).

Appeared Edinburgh Festival with own band, Ronnie and the Rex.

FOTINI DIMOU (designer)

For the Royal Court: Sore Throats, Some Singing Blood.

Other theatre designs include: The Crucible, The Castle, The Archbishop's Ceiling, Fashion, The Storm, Speculators, The Duchess of Malfi, A Jovial Crew, The School of Night (RSC); Principia Scriptoriae (RSC/costumes only); Request Programme (Donmar & Bush); Julius Caesar (Bristol Old Vic); A Child in the Heart (Joint Stock); The Secret Rapture (RNT/costumes only); The House of Blue Leaves (Lilian Baylis Theatre); Sunsets and Glories (West Yorkshire Playhouse); The Seagull (costume design, future project for the RNT); The Lady From the Sea (Riverside Studios & National Theatre of Norway). Extensive work in USA & Athens.

Opera designs include: Blood Wedding (Women's Playhouse Trust); Eugene Onegin (ENO).

Dance designs include: Blue Door, In Dream I Dream A Dream (London Contemporary Dance Theatre); Mysteries (Arc Dance Company); The Rite of Spring (Geneva Ballet); White Nights (English National Ballet).

Films include: The Browning Version (costumes only); 2 short dance films.

IAN DURY (lyrics)

For the Royal Court: Serious Money, Apples.

Other theatre music includes: A Jovial Crew, The Country Wife (RSC).

Films include (as actor): Pirates; The Cook, The Thief, His Wife and Her Lover.

Bands include: Kilburn and the High Roads, The Blockheads.

Records include: New Boots and Panties, What a Waste, Reasons to be Cheerful, Billericay Dickie, Sex and Drugs and Rock and Roll.

PAM FERRIS

For the Royal Court: Devil's Gateway, The Grace of Mary Traverse, Apples, Lucky Chance.

Other theatre includes: Joseph and his Amazing Technicolor Dreamcoat, Armstrong's Last Goodnight, Romeo and Juliet, Jack the Ripper, Caucasian Chalk Circle, No More Sitting on the Old School Bench, Country Wife (Crucible, Sheffield); Arabian Nights, Bleak House, Science Fictions, Cymbeline, La Ronde (Shared Experience); Absent Friends (Bristol Old Vic); Women Beware Women, The Cherry Orchard, The Seagull (Oxford Theatre Co); Having a Ball (Lyric, Hammersmith); Cat on a Hot Tin Roof, Bluebird of Unhappiness, Ridley Walker (Royal Exchange, Manchester); Exclusive Yarns (Watford); The Road to Mecca (Omaha, Nebraska); Roots (RNT & tour); Under the Stars (Greenwich).

TV includes: Miss Julie, Connie, The Bill, Casualty, Lizzie's Pictures, Ladies in Charge, Hardwick House, Sense of Guilt, Oranges are not the Only Fruit, Darling Buds of May, Roots, Sisters, The Blues, Mr. Wakesfield's Crusade, All Change, Middlemarch, The Rector's Wife.

Films include: Winnie, The House, Meantime.

RICK FISHER (lighting designer)

For the Royal Court: Hysteria (Olivier award-winner 1993), King Lear, Six Degrees of Separation (& Comedy); Three Birds Alighting on a Field (1991 & 1992); Serious Money (also West End & Broadway); Bloody Poetry, Rose English (Barclays New Stages), A Mouthful of Birds, A Rock in Water.

Other recent theatre includes: Moonlight (Almeida & Comedy); Misha's Party, All's Well That Ends Well, Elgar's Rondo, Artists and Admirers, The Alchemist, The Virtuoso, 'Tis Pity She's a Whore, Temptation, Restoration, Two Shakespearian Actors (RSC); Some Americans Abroad (RSC & Broadway); The Gift of the Gorgon (RSC & Wyndham's); Machinal, The Coup, Black Snow, Peer Gynt (RNT); An Inspector Calls (RNT & Aldwych); Fiddler on the Roof (West Yorkshire Playhouse); The Crucible (Sheffield Crucible).

Opera lighting includes: Gloriana (Opera North & ROH); Peter Grimes, l'Etoile, La Boheme (Opera North); Manon Lescaut (Dublin); three seasons at Batignano, Italy.

Dance lighting includes: The Kosh, Adventures in Motion Pictures.

MICKEY GALLAGHER (composer)

For the Royal Court: Serious Money, Apples.

Other theatre music includes: A Jovial Crew, The Country Wife (RSC).

Has worked with many notable British hands; co-founder of The Blockheads.

GILLIAN HANNA

For the Royal Court: Hot Fudge and Ice Cream.

Other theatre includes: Sweeney Todd (Liverpool Playhouse); Origin of the Species (Monstrous Regiment/ Birmingham Rep); Sweeney Todd, Destiny, Spend Spend Spend, Elizabeth, Almost by Chance a Woman (Half Moon); Duet for One, Wuthering Heights, Who's Afraid of Virginia Woolf?, A Common Woman, Leonce and Lena (Crucible, Sheffield); The House of Bernarda Alba (Globe and Lyric Hammersmith); Curtains (Hampstead); Love Story of the Century (Monstrous Regiment tour); Juno and the Paycock (Contact, Manchester); Wallflowering (West Yorkshire Playhouse); Romeo and Juliet, A View from the Bridge (Royal Exchange, Manchester); Big Maggie (Birmingham Rep).

TV includes: Brookside, The House of Bernarda Alba, Poirot, The Story of Phillip Knight, Desmonds.

Films include: The Wolves of Willoughby Chase, The Woman of the Wolf.

Books include: Monstrous Regiment, A Collective Celebration.

Translations include: Elizabeth Almost by Chance a Woman, Accidental Death of an Anarchist, A Woman Alone (Dario Fo and Franca Rame).

CAROLE HAYMAN

For the Royal Court: As Time Goes By, Elizabeth I, Wheelchair Willie, Cloud Nine, Top Girls, Ice Cream, Sugar and Spice, Magnificence, Speakers, Light

Shining in Buckinghamshire, Disneyland it Ain't (amongst others).

Directed for the Royal Court: Bazaar and Rummage, The Great Celestial Cow, Byrthrite, Shirley (amongst others)

Other theatre includes work with: Bristol Old Vic, Traverse Theatre Workshop (Edinburgh), Joint Stock Theatre Company, RSC

TV includes: Upline, Howards Way, Dancers, Lytton's Diary, Happy Families, The Lenny Henry Show, Thriller, Within These Walls, Send in the Girls, Not for the Likes of Us, Roger Doesn't Live Here Any More, The Art of Coarse Acting, Cottage to Let, Angels, Hunters Walk, Little Lord Fauntleroy, Jackanory, Courtroom Dramas, Vanity Fair, Jemima Shaw Investigates, Widows, Never Say Die, The Refuge, Born Kicking, Rides.

Films include: Lady Jane, Demon in My View.

Radio includes: hundreds of plays, morning stories, features, Books at Bedtime.

Writing includes: The Refugee (Channel Four); Rides (BBC TV); All the Best Kim (BBC Radio).

Books include: All the Best Kim, Ciao Kim, How the Vote was Won, The Joint Stock Book.

DAVID HOWEY

For the Royal Court: Psy-Warriors, Please Shine Down on Me, An Honourable Trade. Other theatre includes: Third Flight (Bush); St. Joan (Cambridge Theatre Co tour); Good (RSC / Aldwych & Broadway); Educating Rita (Crucible, Sheffield); A Little Like Drowning (Hampstead); Fire in the Lake (Joint Stock tour); As You Like It, Edward II, The Country Wife, (Royal Exchange, Manchester); Fashion, The Revenger's Tragedy, Measure for Measure, The Three Sisters, Titus Andronicus (RSC); Prin (Lyric, Hammersmith & Lyric, West End); Being at Home with Claude (King's Head & Vaudeville); Green Fingers (King's Head). TV includes: Brideshead Revisited, Hang Ups, Yes Minister, Paradise Postponed, Bergerac, Hannay, Just Another Secret, A Wanted Man, Who Bombed Birmingham, Tecx, Jazz Detective, Birds of a Feather, Paul Merton - The Series, Inspector Morse, The Darling Buds of May, Spender, Natural Lies, Minder, No Final Truth, The Life and Times of Henry Pratt, Full Stretch, Harry.

Films include: Rough Cut, Number One, Young Indy.

SUE LEFTON (movement director)

Trained dancer & actor. Currently Head of Movement at Guildhall School of Music & Drama.

Theatre includes: Henry IV Parts I and II, Twelfth Night, The Virtuoso, 'Tis Pity She's a Whore, Romeo and Juliet, The Thebans, The Taming of the Shrew, A Jovial Crew, The Winter's Tale, Hamlet, King Lear, The Country Wife (RSC); Larkrise (Leicester Haymarket, Almeida); Nana (Shared Experience tour, Almeida, Mermaid); A Tale of Two Cities (Cambridge Theatre Company, Tyne & Wear Theatre tour). Has worked with RSC, RNT, Royal Court, Glasgow Citizens' Theatre, Manchester Royal Exchange, Shared Experience, Cambridge Theatre Company.

TV and film includes: Tess (film); major TV series.

Opera includes: Dr. Faust (ENO); frequent work with Jonathan Miller.

JOHN A. LEONARD (sound designer)

UK theatre sound work includes: Royal Court, RSC, RNT, Bristol Old Vic, Manchester Royal Exchange; Almeida, Hampstead, The Old Vic.

Opera includes: ENO.

Other work includes: Madame Tussaud's.

Also worked in Europe & USA.

DOON MACKICHAN

For the Royal Court: Killers.

Other theatre includes: A Midsummer Night's Dream, A Chorus of Disapproval, To Kill a Mockingbird (Birmingham Rep); Bedroom Farce (Bolton Octagon); Dirty Dishes (Boulevard Theatre); Blood Wedding (Buxton Octagon); Troilus and Cressida (Sunday Times Festival); Bogart (Canal Cafe Theatre); Jack and the Beanstalk (Duke's, Lancaster); The Square (BAC); Abigail's Party (Cambridge Theatre & tour); Me and My Friend (Minerva Studio, Chichester).

TV includes: The Day Today, Nothing Like a Royal Show, Off the Wall, Croquet, First Exposure, Dirty Dishes, Wake Up London, Five Alive, Hale and Pace Xmas Extravaganza, The Mary Whitehouse

Experience, Birds of a Feather, The Harry Enfield Show, The Last Laugh, London's Burning, Flip, Sean's Show; For the Comic Strip: The Crying Game, Red Nose of Courage, Space Virgins from the Planet Sex, Detectives on the Edge of a Nervous Breakdown, Gregory Diary of a Nutcase. Radio includes: Death Look, The Mary Whitehouse Experience, Cabaret Upstairs, Rabbitt and Doon, On the Hour, The Nick Revell Show, Knowing Me Knowing You, Down Your Way. Cabaret includes: A Bit of Fluff in Your Gussett (Edinburgh Festival).

PAUL J. MEDFORD

Theatre includes: Fashion (Leicester Haymarket); Hair (Old Vic); Dragon, Bartholomew Fair, The Changeling (RNT); Five Guys Named Moe (Lyric, West End. Olivier nomination for best actor in a musical); Robeson (Young Vic); Cinderella (Shaw Theatre), Salsa Celestina (Watford Palace), Mr Wonderful (Drury Lane)
TV includes: Eastenders, Ghost Train; What's Your Story, House Party, Jimmy Cricket, Something Wrong in Paradise, Minder, The Professionals, The Six o' Clock Show.
Films include: Black Joy, Yesterday's Hero, The Great Muppet Caper.

PEARCE QUIGLEY

For the Royal Court: Downfall, Etta Jenks.
Other theatre includes: A Jovial Crew, A Winter's Tale, Merry Wives of Windsor, The Changeling (RSC); Rope, The Pied Piper (Birmingham Rep); The Tutor/Der Neue Menoza (Gate Theatre); Cider with Rosie, Lady from the Sea, Twelfth Night, The Good Woman of Schezuan, Salonika (Duke's, Lancaster); The Park (Crucible, Sheffield); School for Clowns (Sadler's Wells); Abingdon Square (RNT); Hot Fudge and Ice Cream (Contact, Manchester); Lives of the Great Poisoners (Second Stride).
TV and film includes: Inspector Morse, Killing Dad, Ladder of Swords, A Perfect Hero, Growing Rich, Prime Suspect 3, How to Speak Japanese.
Radio includes: The Fancy Man, Two Planks and a Passion.

TOBY SALAMAN

For the Royal Court: In the Blood, Cinders, Operation Bad Apple, The Hitch-Hiker, Victory (& tour).
Other theatre includes: The Recruiting Officer (Royal Lyceum); Three Sisters (Wolsey, Ipswich); A Free Country (Tricycle); School for Scandal (Bristol Old Vic); Julius Caesar (RSC/Newcastle); Ghosts (Hampstead); The Speakers (ICA & tour); Fanshen (Hampstead & tour); Love of a Good Man, Three Sisters, A Passion in Six Days (Crucible, Sheffield); Two Planks and a Passion (Greenwich); Three Sisters (Shared Experience); The Alchemist (Cambridge Theatre Co); Faith, Hope & Charity (Lyric, Hammersmith).
TV includes: Little Napoleons, Her Majesty's Pleasure, Between the Lines, Love Hurts, Soldier Soldier, Big Battalions, Able's Will, One Day at a Time, Shall I See You Now, The Devil's Crown, One Fine Day, High Tide, Holocaust, Speed King, Mackenzie, World's End, Beyond the Glass, Nelly's Version, The Gathering Seed, Pericles, Jesus, The Evidence, Love Song, The Insurance Man, Tandoori Nights, The Bill.
Films include: Voyage of the Damned, A Bridge Too Far, Sweeney II, The Nativity, The Corsican Brothers, Mission Critical, A World Apart.

MAX STAFFORD-CLARK

Max Stafford-Clark is Artistic Director of Out of Joint, Associate Director at the Royal Court and a Resident Director for the RSC.

JOHANNA TOWN (lighting designer)

For the Royal Court: The Kitchen, Hammett's Apprentice, The Terrible Voice of Satan, Search and Destroy, Women Laughing, Faith Healer, A Jamaican Airman Foresees His Death.
Other lighting designs include: The Lodger, Richard II (Manchester Royal Exchange); Snow Orchid (London Gay Theatre); The Set-Up, Crackwalker (Gate Theatre); Josephine (BAC); Celestina (ATC); Beautiful Thing (Bush and Donmar Warehouse); Macbeth, The Beaux Stratagem (Liverpool Playhouse); The Marriage of Figaro, Eugene Onegin, The Abduction from the Seraglio (Opera 80). Currently Chief Electrician at the Royal Court.

HOW THE ROYAL COURT IS BROUGHT TO YOU...

The English Stage Company at the Royal Court Theatre is supported financially by a wide range of public bodies and private companies, as well as its own trading activities. The theatre receives its principal funding from the **Arts Council of Great Britain**, which has supported the Royal Court since 1956. The **Royal Borough of Kensington & Chelsea** gives an annual grant to the Royal Court Young People's Theatre and provides some of its staff. The **London Boroughs Grants Committee** contributes to the cost of productions in the Theatre Upstairs.

Other parts of the Royal Court's activities are made possible by business sponsorships. Several of these sponsors have made a long term commitment. 1994 has seen the fourth Barclays New Stages Festival of independent theatre, which has been supported throughout by **Barclays Bank**. **British Gas North Thames** has so far supported three years of the Royal Court's Education Programme. Now in its 26th year, the Young Writers' Festival has been sponsored by **Marks and Spencer** since 1991. The latest sponsorship by **WH Smith** has been to help make the launch of the new Friends of the Royal Court scheme so successful.

In 1988 the Royal Court launched the **Olivier Building Appeal** to raise funds to restore, repair and improve the theatre building. So far nearly £700,000 has been raised. The theatre has new bars and front of house areas, new roofs, air conditioning and central heating boilers, a rehearsal room and the theatre's facade has been restored and cleaned. This would not have been possible without a very large number of generous supporters and significant contributions from the **Theatres' Restoration Fund**, the **Rayne Foundation**, the **Foundation for Sport and the Arts** and the **Arts Council's Incentive Funding Scheme**.

The **Gerald Chapman Award** was founded in 1988 to train and develop young theatre directors. It is now jointly funded by the Royal Court and **BBC Television**. The **ITV Companies** fund the **Regional Theatre Young Directors Scheme**, with which the Royal Court has been associated for many years.

1993 saw the start of a new association with the **Audrey Skirball-Kenis Theatre** of Los Angeles. The Skirball Foundation is funding a Playwrights Programme at the Royal Court. Exchange visits for writers between Britain and the USA complement the greatly increased programme of reading and workshops which have fortified the Royal Court's capability to develop new plays.

The Royal Court earns the rest of money it needs to operate from the Box Office, from other trading and from the transfers of plays such as **Death and the Maiden**, **Six Degrees of Separation** and **Oleanna** to the West End. But without public subsidy it would close immediately and its unique place in British Theatre would be lost. The Arts Council has had its grant from the government cut by £3.9 million. This will certainly mean large cuts and reductions in the amount of subsidised theatre activity. If you care about the future of arts in this country, please write to your MP and say so.

THE OLIVIER BUILDING APPEAL

The Royal Court reached the ripe old age of 100 in September 1988. The theatre was showing its age somewhat, and the centenary was celebrated by the launch of the Olivier Appeal, for £800,000 to repair and improve the building.

*Laurence Olivier's long association with the Court began as a schoolboy. He was given "a splendid seat in the Dress Circle" to see his first Shakespeare, **Henry IV Part 2** and was later to appear as Malcolm in **Macbeth** (in modern dress) in a Barry Jackson production, visiting from the Birmingham Repertory Theatre in 1928. His line of parts also included the Lord in the Prologue of **The Taming of the Shrew**. This early connection and his astonishing return in **The Entertainer,** which changed the direction of his career in 1957, made it natural that he should be the Appeal Patron. After his death, Joan Plowright CBE, the Lady Olivier, consented to take over as Patron.*

We are now in sight of our target. With the generous gifts of our many friends and donors, and an award from the Arts Council's Incentive Fund, we have enlarged and redecorated the bars and front of house areas, installed a new central heating boiler and new air conditioning equipment in both theatres, rewired many parts of the building, redecorated the dressing rooms and we are gradually upgrading the lighting and sound equipment.

With the help of the Theatre Restoration Fund, work has now been completed on building a rehearsal room and replacing the ancient roofs. The Foundation for Sport and the Arts have provided a grant which has enabled us to restore the faded Victorian facade of the theatre. So, much is being done, but much remains to do, to improve the technical facilities backstage which will open up new possibilities for our set designers.

*Can you help? A tour of the theatre, including its more picturesque parts, can be arranged by ringing Catherine King on **071 730 5174**. If you would like to help with an event or a gift please ring Graham Cowley, General Manager, on the same number.*

'Secure the Theatre's future, and take it forward towards the new century. For the health of the whole theatrical life of Britain it is essential that this greatly all-providing theatre we love so much and wish so well continues to prosper.'
Laurence Olivier (1988)

Lawrence Olivier 1907-1989
Photo: Snowdon

THE ROYAL COURT THEATRE

The Queen and Ï:

The Play with Songs

Production Note

Harris, the Queen's corgi, was a glove puppet in the first production of the play. He was manipulated by whoever was holding him and his barks, growls and whines were also provided by whoever was holding him.

Clinton, Leanne's baby, was also a puppet in the first production. His crying and whining was provided for by Leanne.

The Lost Boys (some of whom may be girls) played in half-masks in the first production. The leader of the Lost Boys is Karl, the only one to be referred to by name. The speeches by the Lost Boys may be spoken individually, or in two's, three's, four's, or collectively, as the production demands.

Note on Text

When reading the play, bear in mind that some of the lines overlap in performance.

The playscript went to press before the production opened at the Royal Court, London. It may, therefore, differ slightly from the performed play.

The Queen and I: The Play with Songs is a work of dramatic fiction. Names, characters, places and incidents are either the product of the author's imagination or are used entirely fictitiously.

Act One

Scene One

Hell Close at dusk

The **Queen**, **Prince Philip**, **Princess Margaret**, **Diana**, **Charles**, **William** *and the* **Queen Mother** *enter, carrying bags. The* **Queen** *is carrying* **Harris**, *her Corgi dog.*

Queen This can't be it.

Margaret We're obviously in the wrong place. Nobody could live in those ghastly little houses.

Philip It *is* the wrong bloody place! This is *Hell* Close and we want *Hellebore*. Where's the bloody map?

Charles Diana, where's the map?

Diana I dunno, you had it last.

Charles No. I gave it back to you at Junction 21.

Diana You did not! You snatched it out of my hand at that roundabout thingy!

Charles Only because you couldn't find the Oadby bloody turn off.

Diana You said nothing about Oadby. You were screaming about the B406.

Philip It's in your pocket, boy! Hurry up, I'm due to go to the lavatory in five minutes.

Charles *gets the map out and looks at it.*

Queen Mother There's a horrid smell isn't there?

Queen (to **Queen Mother**) Sit down while we sort this out, darling.

William Can we go, Mummy? I hate it here.

Diana Yes, Wills darling. Just as soon as Pa has finished looking at his silly map.

Charles It isn't a silly map, Diana, it's just that you're totally incapable of reading the bloody thing!

Margaret Why should she be skilled at map reading? One doesn't need a map to find one's wardrobe.

Diana You think I'm thick, don't you?

Queen You did once announce to the world's media that you were as thick as two short planks, Diana.

Diana That was before I'd seen two short planks.

Philip God all bloody mighty! What's that on my bloody shoe?

Charles It looks like er . . . dog faeces, Pa.

Diana People call it *shit* Charles. Dog *shit!*

Queen Mother Why is Diana being so vŭlgar, Lilibet?

Queen We're all tired and a little overwrought. But please! Not in front of William.

William Actually, we call it dog shit at school, Granny.

Queen Charles! I'd like to leave here before it gets dark. Concentrate on the map will you please darling.

Charles Well er . . . according to the map this *is* Hellebore Close.

Queen It can't be, darling.

Charles I'm afraid it is.

Diana We can't live here.

Margaret It's like Goblin's Wood.

Queen Mother Without the trees.

Leanne *comes on pushing her little boy* **Clinton** *who is whining.*

Leanne Shurrup whining. You're doing my faxin' head in Clinton.

Charles Er . . . excuse me, madam.

Leanne I can't pay you until Friday.

Charles I beg your pardon?

Leanne An' any road, I don't see why I should pay you *owt*, the wheels 'ave fell off twice.

Charles It's not money I want from you. It's, er, your local wisdom.

Leanne You're not from the finance then?

Charles No.

Queen We're looking for Hellebore Close.

Leanne This is it. The kids 'ave buggered the sign up, so it's *Hell* Close now. Suits it better anyroad. It is hell living round here an' all.

Margaret (*to* **Leanne**) I wonder, could I trouble you for a cigarette?

Leanne (*to* **Margaret**) I can't, this is me last one. (*To* **Charles**.) I know you from somewhere.

Margaret I must find a tobacconist.

Queen But you're a non-smoker now, Margot!

Margaret The next time you see me I shall be smoking from every visible orifice, Lilibet.

Queen Mother Leave her be Lilibet. Everybody should have a hobby.

Charles Thank you so much Mrs. . . ?

Leanne Jus' call me Leanne.

Charles Just call me Charlie, Leanne.

He holds out his hand. **Leanne** *takes it.* **Charles** *holds it a fraction longer than is normal.*

Leanne Your 'ands are dead soft. It's a long time since *you* worked, en't it?

Leanne *exits.*

Queen Our house is number 45, Philip. Diana is in 27, and your bungalow is just round the corner Mummy, quite near to Margot.

Philip We can't live in *this* street, woman!

Queen Mother This has been a most interesting outing. But I would like to go back to Clarence House now.

William Mummy, take me home! Please! Please!

Diana Charles, William is petrified. We can't live here.

Charles It's too late, the people have spoken, Diana.

Queen Mother What people, darling?

Charles This is a democracy, Granny. And, er, in a . . .

Philip Democracy! I don't give an elephant's ball for democracy! Where were the bloody military when we needed them eh?

Charles But Pa, we must look on this as an opportunity to find out who we really are. I must confess I find the prospect immensely exciting. A sapling planted here, a bottle bank there, perhaps a maypole.

Diana & Philip Oh shut up, Charles!

Diana It'll take more than a maypole to make me happy.

Queen Mother Are we really to stay here forever?

Diana (*crying*) Yes Granny! Poor Wills in this horrendous environment, and no money!

Queen Mother No money! But how will I pay the servants?

Queen You won't need servants, Mummy. You'll have a nice little bungalow, and you'll get a pension book.

Queen Mother Oh, I shall look forward to that! I shall have to buy a purse shan't I?

The **Queen** *walks over to number 45.*

Queen This is our new home, Philip.

Philip There's a bloody tree growing in the gutter!

Queen It's a very small tree.

Charles A sycamore. They seed very easily.

Philip I refuse! I abso-bloody-lutely refuse!

Queen Philip! I'm tired and hungry and I don't like it out here in the street. Open the door please. You have the key.

Queen Mother I shall buy a *red* purse. One with a special compartment for coins.

Philip *examines the door.*

Philip The bloody door's boarded up. Need a tool of some kind.

Queen There may be something in the pantechnicon. Come on, we must stay together.

The Royals start to walk off, **William** *holds* **Charles***'s hand.*

William Pa, you'll stay with me and Mummy tonight won't you?

Charles Wills darling, you know I can't, Mummy and I are separated. I've been allocated a single person flat.

William Oh Pa! I can't bear it.

Charles It's on the ground floor, it's got a garden.

Diana And he'll be out there digging in the bloody dark, while we get murdered in our beds.

The door to number 43 opens. **Violet Toby** *puts milk bottles onto the step. She watches as the Royal Family walk off.* **Violet** *lights a cigarette and stands with her arms folded surveying her territory.*

Violet I'm Violet Toby. I run things round 'ere. It's me who started the Pensioners' Dinner Club, and takes 'em to Skeggy in the summer. I can make a weddin' dress, drive a lorry, deliver a baby and wrestle any man in 'Ell Close to the ground. But I 'ave 'ad bad luck wi' men. When I married me fourth, Wilf, 'e 'ad a decent set o' lungs, an' a job with the Gas Board. Now 'e's outa work, an' 'is lungs are kept goin' by the National Health. Two minutes of sex an' 'e's buggered. That's no good to me. Don't get me wrong, I'd do owt for 'im. It's jus' that I like a bloke who goes out in the morning and comes back at night. And I like a wage packet on the table on Friday night. A wage packet puts lead in a bloke's pencil. A giro don't. A giro don't satisfy nobody. It ain't big enough. Size does count.

The **Queen**, **Prince Philip**, **Diana**, **William**, **Prince Charles** *and the* **Queen Mother** *come on.* **Philip** *and* **Charles** *are carrying a large rolled-up carpet. They grunt and groan as they carry it along the pavement.*

Violet Movin' in?

Queen Yes.

Violet I'm your next door neighbour then. Violet Toby.

Queen How do you do? Have you been waiting long?

Violet I'm not waiting, I live 'ere.

Queen And for how many years have you lived here?

Violet Twenty-seven.

Queen Really? How very interesting.

Violet Interestin'? I wun't say that.

Queen And does your family live with you?

Charles Mummy you don't have to . . . do it any more.

Queen Do what?

Charles The talk. The 'How long have you been waiting' sort of stuff.

Queen Thank you, Charles. (*To* **Violet**.) Would you have an *axe* I could borrow?

Violet An *ix*?

Queen Yes, an *axe*.

Violet I dunno what an *ix* is.

Queen You don't know what an *axe* is?

Violet No, worrisit?

Queen Worrisit?

Violet Yeah. Worrisit. Wossanix?

Queen Wossan ix?

Violet Worrisit you want?

Diana Does your husband have a *chopper*?

Violet He had one the last time I looked, yeah.

Philip We need an implement to gain access to our house.

Violet To your *arse*?

Philip *House* woman, *house*! The front door!

Violet (*shouting*) Wilf! Pass us the chopper. (*She points a finger at* **Philip**.) Don't call me 'woman' again.

Violet (*to* **Queen**) You know who you look like? That woman what impersonates the Queen. I seen 'er when she opened that new frozen food place, 'Penguin's Palace'.

The axe is passed to **Violet**. *She goes to number 45 and starts to prise the grille off the front door.*

Queen Really, how very fascinating.

Violet You talk like 'er an' all. You should go on the clubs. All you'd need is a long frock an' a crown from a joke shop.

Queen I am, was, the Queen. We are, were, used to be, the Royal Family.

Violet *is stunned.*

Violet Right. (*Pause.*) Right. (*Pause.*) Right. (*Pause.*) So. I seen the removal vans leavin' the Palace, it were on the telly. David Dimbleby were cryin' his bleddy eyes out.

Philip (*looking at his watch*) Lavatory!

He rushes into number 45.

Queen It does seem rather harsh.

Charles Better than being put up against a wall and shot.

Queen Only marginally better, I think.

Violet (*shouting*) Wilf! Wilf! Put yer glasses on, make sure yer zip's done up, an' come out 'ere!

Wilf (*off*) I'm still on the lavvy!

Violet 'E's got an irritable bowel. Well 'e's got an irritable everything really. (*To* **William**.) You're William ain't yer? You'll be goin' to school with my grandson, Craig. 'E's a bleeder 'e is.

William Mummy, I want to stay on at Ludgrove. How is it that Harry can stay there, but not me?

Diana We can't afford for both of you to go to Ludgrove, darling. Harry can only stay for one more term.

William But Granny is the richest woman in the world. She's got billions of pounds.

Violet (*laughing*) Not today she's not. 'Ow much did they give you 'til your benefits come through?

Queen Fifty pounds. A starter box of groceries. And two sort of card/token devices which enable one to obtain gas and electricity.

Violet Not allowed to flog nowt either are you?

Charles It's, er, quite a relief to be rid of one's possessions, actually.

Violet If you don't hurry up and empty that van, you'll have nowt left at all.

The **Queen** *is looking at a spray-painted message on the wall of number 45.*

Queen Charles, your German is better than mine. What does 'Die Bitch' mean? (*She pronounces it 'Dee Bitch'.*)

Violet It ain't German. It says, 'Die Bitch'.

Queen A sort of . . . death threat, is it?

Violet It's nowt to do with you. I done it . . .

Wilf Toby *appears on the doorstep.*

. . . I found 'im . . . (*She slaps* **Wilf**'*s head.*) with his trousers round 'is ankles in next door's airing cupboard. Reckoned he were adjustin' her thermostat. She moved out the nex' day.

Diana That's what I should have done, sprayed 'Die Bitch' on *Camilla*'s front door.

Queen Please Diana!

Violet That carpet'll never fit. Your biggest room's nine by nine.

Wilf *is now wearing his glasses. He is looking at the Royals.*

Wilf Is this 'Beadle's About', Violet?

Violet No, it's really them. Come to live nex' door. (*To* **Charles**.) Take this lot inside. Then go and fetch your bedroom stuff.

Wilf *stares at* **Diana**.

Violet Are you all moving into number 45?

Queen No, just my husband and I.

Violet (*to the* **Queen**) You an' me are the only women in Hell Close oo's still got a bloke livin' with 'em. (*She glares at* **Wilf**.) An' the way he's shapin' up . . . Are you going to try and flog that battery or what? I'm sick of tripping over the bleddy thing.

Wilf I'll tek it later.

Violet Right, form a line an' let's get some of this stuff inside. You go there. Come on, me duck. (*Asking for first item to be passed along.*) Picture.

The Royals form a line and pass the furniture along.

Diana (*to* **Charles**) Do you see what you've done? All I am now is a single parent! I'm a statistic, put out by the Child Poverty Action group.

Queen Diana! Charles has supported you and the boys in the past, and he will continue to do so.

Charles And I'll see William on Sundays.

Diana (*to* **Charles**) You make me sick!

Queen If you must be sick, try to avoid that carpet will you? It was a present to Queen Victoria from the Maharajah of Jaipur, and I'm rather fond of it.

Everyone apart from **Wilf**, **Violet** *and the* **Queen** *is now inside the house.*

The **Queen** *and* **Violet** *are carrying the carpet between them.* **Wilf** *stands watching the proceedings.*

Violet Right, you'll want your beds in next.

The **Queen** *holds her forehead.*

Queen Beds! There isn't a bed for Philip. Where will he sleep tonight?

Violet Wi' you!

Queen Philip, are you all right darling? (*Exits into house.*)

Charles (*re-entering*) Some lads are behind the van with some paintings that are remarkably similar to those owned by one's grandmother.

Violet Thieving scumbags. 'Ere gis that me an' get after them. Quick before they flog 'em.

William I'll help you, Daddy.

Charles *and* **William** *exit.*

Wilf What you 'elpin' 'em for? Ain't it enough that we've paid us taxes to keep 'em in luxury all their lives?

Violet We can't leave 'em like this, Wilf. They're like babies.

Wilf I've never seen owt like it.

Violet Like what?

Wilf Their skin. It's like they're fresh out the packet. We look like chunks a' corned beef by the side a' them. How long do you give 'em?

Violet Not long. It's like sending a family of teddy bears to 'ave a picnic in the jungle.

Wilf We can't have them living round here Violet, we've got enough problem families as it is, we've got a full quota.

Scene Two

The Lost Boys
  Who's hard?
  I'm hard.
  Who's hardest?
  I'm the hardest.

You're the hardest.
You're the hardest.
He's the hardest.
He's the hardest.
(*Looking at a painting.*) Wo's that?
Picture.
Picture.
Posho's picture.
Posho's picture.
Posho's picture.
What do we do with it?
Burn it.
Burn it.
Burn it.
Burn it.
Sell it.
Sell it.
Sell it.
Psssst. Filth.
Psssst.
Pssssst.

Scene Three

The barrier

Inspector Holyland *and* **PC Ludlow** *are standing behind police tape.*

Holyland Ever met royalty, Ludlow?

Ludlow No, Sir.

Holyland I have. Greatest day of my life. I was a mere constable, much like you. Perhaps with a spark more ambition. The Queen Mother came to the County Show, rode round in a carriage, waving, like she does. A good twenty minutes. Ever waved for twenty minutes, Ludlow?

Ludlow No, Sir.

Holyland Looks easy, doesn't it?

Ludlow Yes, it does, Sir.

Holyland Try it sometime. It takes some doing. (*Pause.*) She looked a picture. Periwinkle blue she was wearing. Anyroad she did a walkabout and who did she stop and talk to?

Ludlow I don't know, Sir.

Holyland Me! (*A long pause.*) Don't you want to know what she said to me, and what I said to her?

Ludlow Isn't it confidential, Sir?

Holyland Strictly speaking yes. But we're going back nineteen years, so . . . she came up to me and said. 'How long have you been in the police force?' 'Two years, Ma'am', I said. She sort of ducked her head and said, 'Quite a long time'. (*He smiles to himself.*)

Ludlow Sir, are we keeping *them* in, or other people out?

Holyland Both. Did you vote Republican, Ludlow? I did. Parasites sapping the country's strength, that's your modern Royalty.

Ludlow I didn't vote, Sir.

Holyland You got any politics, Ludlow?

Ludlow No. I haven't got time for politics, me and Wendy are still doing the house up.

Holyland Well just remember, Ludlow, when you do come face to face with royalty, there'll be no kowtowing, no grovelling, we'll maintain our dignity.

Ludlow Omigod Sir! Omigod! Oh Jesus! Look who's coming.

Princess Diana *runs on.*

Diana I want to report a theft, two thefts, two paintings.

Inspector Holyland *bows extravagantly.* **Ludlow** *turns round and round on his heel, his hands over his eyes.*

Ludlow Omigod!

Holyland Good evening Ma'am. May I say how deeply honoured we are to have you living on our patch.

Diana *(smiling)* Well, it's lovely to be here. No, it isn't, is it? We've only just arrived and we've been robbed.

Holyland Paintings you say.

Diana Yes, they're both priceless. One was a sort of Rembrandty thing, and the other was, oh, you know . . . um . . . begins with a 'T'.

Holyland Ludlow, you're artistic. Priceless, begins with a 'T'.

Ludlow Titian?

Diana Yes! How clever.

Ludlow I went to Art College, but I didn't like the uniform . . .

Diana There were some boys, hanging around. They had faces like something out of . . . oh, you know, he was an illustrator . . . begins with an 'H'.

Ludlow Hogarth!

Diana Yes. Faces like that.

Ludlow Sounds like the Lost Boys posse, Sir.

Holyland It does. *(Pause.)*

Diana I shall have to go. I've left William on his own, another lost boy.

Diana *leaves.*

Ludlow *buries his face in his hands.*

Ludlow What am I going to *do*?

Holyland You're going to go round to her house later and take a proper statement.

Ludlow My marriage is *over*! How can I go home to Wendy now that I've met her? She said I was clever. I think I'm in love with her, Sir.

Holyland Ludlow! You're a victim of the tabloids! Once you clap eyes on Wendy with her two-toned spectacles and sensible cardigan you'll realise where your true affections lie.

Princess Margaret *approaches.* **Holyland** *drops to his knees.*

Princess Margaret *comes to the barrier.*

Holyland Good evening, Mrs Armstrong-Jones.

Margaret *tries to get past* **Ludlow** *and* **Holyland**. *They restrain her.*

Margaret Let me through. I'm in desperate need of cigarettes.

Holyland Very sorry, Ma'am, but the ex-Royal Family are restricted to the immediate environs of Hell Close.

Margaret But the tobacconist refuses to deliver and I also need to get to Marks and Spencers. I can't cook. Does the new government want me to starve to death?

Holyland I don't think it's official policy Ma'am.

Margaret I prefer to be addressed as 'Your Royal Highness'.

Holyland Sorry, Your Royal Highness, but 'Your Royal Highness' is now a forbidden form of address.

Ludlow We got a fax this morning, Your Royal Highness.

Margaret I have an engagement tonight with a young man. We were meant to dine *à deux*. Am I allowed to go?

Holyland No, sorry Ma'am, but perhaps I could introduce you to the area, when things ease up a bit. I'm not without culture.

Margaret Perhaps, but you are without youth. (*To* **Ludlow**.) Do you smoke Constable?

Ludlow No.

Spiggy (*off*) Videos!

Ludlow But Spiggy will sell you some fags, Your Royal Highness.

Holyland I'll go and have a chat to the Chief Constable about that Titian, Ludlow.

Holyland *exits*.

Ludlow *keeps an eye on things*.

Spiggy *enters*.

Leanne *enters, pushing* **Clinton**.

Spiggy Videos! Perfect for the kiddios. Come and get your videos. *Rambo One*, *Two*, *Three* and *Four*! Spiggy brings 'em to your door!

Leanne (*to* **Spiggy**) I've gotta complaint! This is faxin' *Bambi*!

Spiggy (*to* **Leanne**) So?

Margaret (*to* **Spiggy**) Could I have a pack of cigarettes please, Mr Spiggy?

Spiggy What sort of fags?

Margaret (*to* **Spiggy**) Those with the most nicotine!

Spiggy Three quid. (*Hands her a packet of Rothmans cigarettes*.)

Leanne (*to* **Spiggy**) So. I asked you for sommat excitin' for 'im!

Spiggy (*to* **Leanne**) It's gotta *fire*! Bambi's mother gets *killed*!

Leanne He likes car chases what end up with an explosion.

Margaret *tears open the packet, and inserts a cigarette into a holder.*

Margaret *Bambi* is terribly sad. I wept for a week.

Leanne Give us sommat from *Elm Street*.

Spiggy *One* or *Two?*

Leanne (*bragging*) *Three*. He seen *One* an' *Two* before.

Margaret *waits for somebody to light her cigarette.*

Spiggy It's out. Did he understand what he was watching?

Leanne Well I wun't know, would I? He cun't talk at nine months could 'e? He can't talk now. 'E jus guz round bitin' people.

Margaret Isn't somebody going to give me a light?

Leanne *gives* **Margaret** *her own cigarette.* **Margaret** *hesitates, then lights her own cigarette from* **Leanne**'*s*

Leanne I want sommat that'll get him to sleep. I'm going out for a drink tonight.

Margaret A drink? How lovely!

Spiggy (*to* **Margaret**) You're the one that *likes* a drink, aren't you?

Leanne Shut the fax up Clinton! Oh gissus *Elm St One* again. Owt to get him to sleep (*To* **Margaret**.) I'm gonna try and find a new dad for him. (*To* **Clinton**.) A nice new dad for you, eh Clinty? An' a nice new 'usband for me. (*To* **Margaret**.) I want one that don't mind taking you shopping. And I wun't go to faxin' Penguin's Palace neither. Come for a drink if you like. I'll be in the Crown.

Margaret Unfortunately, I won't. Which is the story of my life.

Ludlow The Crown's out of bounds to 'em, Leanne.

Spiggy What is it you drink?

Margaret Scotch. Famous Grouse.

Leanne (*to* **Ludlow**) You didn't tell me you'd got married!

Ludlow I forgot!

Spiggy (*pulls out a bottle*) It's scotch, but it's not famous.

Margaret I'll take it.

Spiggy Ten quid. Do you want to place a regular order for some heavy duty fags?

Margaret Yes. Rothmans. You're a sort of peripatetic corner shop are you?

Spiggy I do a bit of everything. I put an engine in a car this morning. I've got a carpet to fit tonight.

Margaret I'm astonished that people can afford cars and carpets. The ghastly place *reeks* of poverty. Is there a place of worship? (*She opens the bottle.*)

Spiggy There's a church, it's covered in razor wire.

Margaret *drinks*.

Margaret I shall pray to the God that ordained my family to deliver me from this hell.

Spiggy You don't know what it used to be like round here, how could you? This estate were planned by elected councillors. Labour men, like myself, and it were a dream come true. Hellebore Close, Primrose Lane, Daisy Gardens, nice names. You were proud to give your address. And there were hosiery and shoe factories nearby. At half-past seven in the morning these pavements were full of people, all going in the same direction, to work. And they were wearing the boots and shoes and socks they'd made themselves.

Ludlow (*to* **Spiggy**) Do you know *The Joy of Lovemaking*?

Margaret I knew it once, Tony was terribly good at it.

Ludlow I was talking to Spiggy, Your Royal Highness.

Spiggy I've got it but it's out with Wilf Toby.

Spiggy *goes off.*

Spiggy (*off*) Videos! Come and get your videos, *Rambo*, *One*, *Two*, *Three* and *Four*, Spiggy brings 'em to your door!

Ludlow I ought to tell you Ma'am, that it's an offence to drink in the street.

Margaret I can't go home sober. I should have been Queen, Constable. Queen Margaret. A white glove, a flash of diamonds as my carriage went by.

She waves drunkenly as **Ludlow** *exits.*

Lost Boys *enter, with painting.*

Lost Boys
  Oi.
  Eh.
  Psssst.
  Five pounds.

Margaret What do you mean? That's our picture.

Lost Boys
  Our picture.
  Our picture.
  Our picture now.

Margaret You don't scare me. I shall tell your parents.

Lost Boys
  Parents.
  Parents.
  No parents.
  No father.
  What's a father?
  What's a dad?
  Sad.
  Sad.
  What's a dad.

Margaret All right. Four pounds.

Lost Boys
 Thank you, Ma'am.
 Thank you.
 Ooooh.
 We're so grateful.
 So grateful.
 So humble and grateful.

Margaret Well, you should be.

Lost Boys
 We should be.
 We should be.
 Yes, we should be.
 But we ain't.

Margaret We could help each other.

Lost Boys
 Help.
 Help.

Margaret You know nothing.

Lost Boys
 We don't know anything.
 Know nothing.
 Stupid.
 Stupid.
 We're stupid.
 No 'O' level.
 No 'A' level.
 Eh?
 Oh?
 Oh?
 Eh?

Margaret Nor me. But I'll buy your picture. You. Come to my house.

Exit **Margaret**.

Lost Boys
> Ohhh.
> Will he come?
> Will she come?
> He'll come
> She'll come.
> She'll come.
> Come to her house.
> Come in her house.

All but two **Lost Boys** *exit.*

Two Lost Boys
> Can't come in my house. Stepdad's drunk.
> Punk, punk, Stepdad's drunk.
> Beats our Mam.
> Wham, bam, beats yer Mam.
> Worstest thing I ever seen.
> Worra frightener for the Queen.

'Domestic and Street' song.

What makes you think I've had a drink I've had a drink a
  bloody drink
This bloody grub's no bloody good it's bloody cold and
  where's my spuds
Oh no you won't . . .

Oh yes I will, oh yes I will, I bloody will
We'll see about that you little prat you're asking to get killed.
Oh no you don't, now put it down, you're making me get
  cross

Go on my son give her some stick, go on my son give her
  some faxing stick

You'll never learn you silly cow, I'll show you who's the boss

Oh get your bloody hands off me off me off me get off

Come here you bitch you bloody witch I'll shove you in the
  trough

Oy you drunken bastard, leave that girl alone you drunken –

Have some of that, ahh, have some of that, ooh!
Smack, ouch! Wack, ah! Crack, crack ow!

Get back you slag you bloody hag I'll punch you in the face

Take that you sod I wish to God I had a hiding place

If that's the way you want to play I'll smash you in the chops

I hope to God I hope to God I hope it bloody stops

You raise your hand to me once more I won't be held to
    blame

Now count to ten and say amen you all the bloody same

There's wilful murders going on at number 43

Thank you my dear, you stay right here, I'll go and have a
    see
Alpha Foxtrot Able Baker George Over and out calling in
    10–4

Fax off copper! (Etc. . . .)

And I'm going in. This is me going in. Allo allo allo, what's
    going hon 'ere?

Have some of that, aah! Have some of that, ooh!
Smack, ouch! Wack, ah! Crack, crack ow!
Have some of this, oof! Have some of this, umpf!
Kick, aww! Stick, oh! Flick, flick aaee!

He ain't a pit bull he's a staff, got six more like him round
    my gaff
He got these scars from falling over, go boy go boy go boy
    Rover

The situation here it's all gone off down here
Come along in numbers and wear your riot gear
She would have killed him but I stopped her, where the hell's
    that helicopter?

It's over there it's over there

There's a transit full of cops, now it's burning and it stops
As the flames begin to spout, watch the bogies tumble out

Here we go, here we go, here we go oh oh oh oh
You what you what you what you what you what what what
    what what?

There's a sergeant here's a brick, chuck it at him double
    quick
Now he's lost his rotten hat, job him with a baseball bat

Final chorus: Have some of that, aah! (Etc   .)

End of song.

Scene Four

Next morning – Queen's kitchen

Violet *is showing the* **Queen** *how to boil an egg.*

Violet So, 'ow does 'e like 'is eggs then, Mrs Windsor?

Queen Soft. I think. With his bread and butter cut up into
soldiers.

Violet Well, he's a military man isn't he?

Queen Not at the moment he isn't, Mrs Toby. He said he
won't get out of bed until the central heating has warmed the
house.

Violet 'E'll be in bed a long time then. You've *got* no central
'eating.

Queen (*alarmed*) But that switch next to that tank thing!
Isn't that . . . ?

Violet (*cutting in*) That's your *immersion* for your hot water.

Queen And the hot water doesn't circulate?

Violet The only thing that circulates round these 'ouses is *rumours*. Right, get a spoon and lift the egg out the pan, Mrs Windsor. No, not a teaspoon! A big un!

Queen What a fool you must think I am.

Violet Well *I* wun't know 'ow to write a Queen's speech would I?

Queen Oh one didn't *write* it. One simply read the lies one's government wrote for one.

Violet Right, lift it out, an' if the water dries dead quick on the shell, you know it's cooked.

Queen Thank you, Mrs Toby, er . . . when I let Harris out this morning I saw a rat in my back garden.

Violet A *ret*? What's one of them?

Queen A *rat*, a rodent.

Violet Oh a rat! Oh don't worry about them, they don't come in the 'ouses, well hardly, they've got their own complex. Can you do your own bread and butter?

Queen Oh, yes, yes.

Violet Right I'll get off then.

Queen But I am having a more *intimate* difficulty, Mrs Toby.

Violet Intimate?

Queen Yes, the thing is I'm having enormous difficulty in fastening my brassiere.

Violet You can't put your own bra on?

Queen Oh it's on! It's on! But try as I may I can't fasten it. Would you . . . ? Do you think you could . . . ?

Violet (*dubiously*) Fasten it?

Queen Yes.

Violet I couldn't. Sorry..It wouldn't seem right. I mean it were only yesterday you were the Queen. I can't go messin' about wi' yer bra straps. I cun't imagine yer even *wearin'* a bra, or sittin' on the lavvy or owt.

Queen It's awfully uncomfortable.

The **Queen** *pulls at her bra.*

Violet Go on then, come 'ere.

The **Queen** *goes to* **Violet**. **Violet** *pulls the* **Queen**'s *jumper up and gathers the bra straps together at the back.*

Violet What you do is fasten it up round your front first, twist it round, and *then* pull it up over your doo dars. You've kept your figure very nice.

Queen Thank you, but I'm looking forward tremendously to letting it go.

Violet Why din't you ask the Duke to help you?

Queen I'm afraid we had a quarrel this morning. (*Heatedly.*) I've got so much to *do* and he just *lies there*, complaining.

Both women look up.

Violet Wilf took it hard when *he* were made redundant. He left me for three days, he went to Wales.

Queen Wales?

Violet They all go to Wales, eventually.

Queen Who?

Violet The blokes, there's nowt to keep 'em 'ere, is there? There's no work, and the women look after the kids.

Philip *shouts down.*

Philip (*off*) Must I wait *forever* for my breakfast!

Queen (*shouting*) I'm doing the best I can!

Violet I'll leave you t'ave a row in peace. (*She goes to the door.*) You want Penguin's Palace for your frozen stuff, but don't bother with the sausage rolls. Co-op for your milk, Spiggy'll cut your carpets to fit.

Queen My beautiful carpets!

Violet And it's pensioners' dinner three times a week, at the Community Centre.

Queen Thank you, Mrs Toby.

Violet Don't mention it, Mrs Windsor.

Scene Five

Diana's Living Room

Diana *and* **David Dorkin** *are sitting facing each other.* **Dorkin** *is nervous, making no eye contact, fumbling with the catches on his briefcase.*

Diana Would you like a cup of tea, Mr Donkey?

Dorkin *Dorkin*. David Dorkin.

Diana Sorry. And you're from the SS?

Dorkin *D*SS. Department of Social Security. No tea, we're not supposed to . . .

Diana On duty. Like the police . . . fire and ambulance. I suppose you *are* an emergency service . . .

Dorkin We try not to be.

Diana But everybody in Hell Close seems to need your help, nobody seems to have a job.

Dorkin There are jobs for those who want to work.

Diana Are there? I really want a job. What kind of work is available?

Dorkin I know there's a vacancy for a deep-sea sponge diver, but it would probably mean leaving Leicester.

Diana And I'm not allowed to do that. Shame. I'm rather a good diver.

Dorkin I can't swim at all. Sinus trouble. . . . You've applied for a grant for decorating materials?

Diana Wallpaper and paint. William's bedroom is covered in black stuff. And there's a mushroom thing growing in the corner of my bedroom. . . . Do you want to see?

Dorkin Not yet. Just answer a few questions. What's your weekly income?

Diana I don't know. I couldn't work it out. Even with a dictionary and William's calculator.

Dorkin Here's how it works. If you take your Child Benefit and your Single Parent Allowance, and deduct your Housing Benefit but add any Special Needs payment, it works out that you get a weekly mean which *will* allow you to survive but you won't be living high on the hog. Do you understand?

Diana High on the hog? . . . Sorry . . . (*Laughing.*) No, I must be thick or something. So how much will I get, a week?

Dorkin I'm not able to facilitate an answer. The computer's down.

Diana Only you see it would be quite sort of convenient to know. My husband and I are separated. So I'm completely dependent on you, Mr Dorkin. I suppose I'm married to the State now, aren't I?

Dorkin *writes.* **Diana** *watches anxiously.*

Dorkin Not married, but you're certainly co-habiting. (*Laugh.*)

Diana Mr Dorkin, you haven't looked at me once. Is there something wrong?

Dorkin Sorry. I'm a bit at sea. My training didn't equip me for dealing with A/B categories.

Diana So this is difficult for you, is it?

Dorkin Yes. I'm used to working with the old and the ugly, the sick and the lame.

Diana Poor things. Do you want to come upstairs and see the damp patch and the mushroom?

Dorkin Yes.

Diana I won't be a moment. I'll just go and tidy a few things away.

Diana *exits*.

Dorkin (*straight-faced*) I'd love to go upstairs with you. To see for myself. To kiss you, and lay you down on your damp bed. If you want to decorate your room in gold leaf, I'll find the money for it. I'll take it from the pensioners' cold weather allowance.

Diana *hasn't heard* **Dorkin***'s speech*.

Dorkin *stands and sees a pair of men's shoes on the floor. He picks them up*.

Dorkin (*shouts upstairs*) Who do these belong to?

Diana (*entering*) Charles.

Dorkin But you've made separate applications for Supplementary Benefit.

Diana We don't live together. He only stayed for one night.

Dorkin Did you share a bed with him?

Diana I was forced to!

Dorkin Forced you did he.

Diana There wasn't a spare bed you see.

Dorkin Now we come to the crucial point. The right or wrong answer could make quite a big difference to your weekly benefit. Couples who live together receive a lot less money so bear that in mind. Was there *movement* in the bed?

Diana Yes, it's quite a springy mattress. But why do you ask?

Dorkin I'll put it more clearly. Were your and his relations *intimate*?

Diana (*sadly*) No. Our relations have never really got on. I've got Barbara Cartland as a step-grandmother you know.

Dorkin You've forced me to use the words. Did you enjoy sexual intercourse with your husband?

Diana I've never enjoyed sexual intercourse with anybody. This is a terrible invasion of privacy. You're making me blush.

Dorkin So is your answer yes or no? The State has given me power to insist upon an answer. I've got to write something down.

Diana I don't know Mr Dorkin, what do you think?

Dorkin I think: No. Now, if you'll show me that mushroom.

They go upstairs.

Scene Six

Queen Mother's Living Room

Philomena Toussaint *and the* **Queen Mother** *are looking through their photograph albums.* **Philomena** *is wearing her hat and coat.*

Queen Mother And who are these splendid-looking chaps, Mrs Toussaint?

Philomena Me boys, that's Fitzroy, that's Curtis, that's Eugene. They being baptised on the beach. That's Archbishop Percy. Good boys. They never bring no trouble to the house. I must go to me bed soon.

Queen Mother But it's only four o'clock.

Philomena Me bedtime is five o'clock. I can't afford to heat me room after that.

Queen Mother I've got some adorable photographs of my girls as babies. Look, this is them with Crawfie their nurse.

Queen Mother's and Mrs Toussaint's song.

Queen Mother
  Golly made wonderful cakes
  With horseshoes and bells and bright silver pills
  It's odd how the memory awakes

Philomena
  In the sunset at Montego Bay
  With Archbishop Percy and the Sisters of Mercy
  And we're singing on Michaelmas Day

Queen Mother
  As old as the silver of wisdom

Philomena
  My Kingston farewell

Queen Mother
  As young as the face of a smile

Philomena
  Wipe the tears from my eyes

Queen Mother
  As warm as the memory of happier times

Philomena
  Happier times

Both
This is me when I was a child

Queen Mother
Here's Bertie and I playing cards
And quite a good snap of a pony and trap
Margaret Rose with some Grenadier Guards

Philomena
Here I am on the Saffron Estate
That's Fitzroy and me on the Queen's Jubilee
Oh the street celebrations were great

Philomena
Ennobled by former creation

Queen Mother
What time won't dispel

Philomena
And noble in manner and style

Queen Mother
The heart beautifies

Philomena
Here's to the memory of happier times

Queen Mother
Happier times

Both
As it was when I was a child

Both
The older I am, the younger I feel
May God bless the children, eating their meal
When the flag of an Empire, proclaimed an ideal
The sun sets at six on the sugar cane field

Queen Mother
Here the children are playing sardines, and look

At you Ma'am. My grey Lady of Glamis
Margaret Rose with some Royal Marines

Philomena
Oh that ship was so rusty and old
Here my husband meets me at Southampton on Sea
And then London so filthy and cold

Both
And here we both are in the prime of our lives
Near that time of our lives when our moment arrives
So here's to the health of the mothers and wives
And long may their spirit survive

End of song.

Queen Mother Do, please, take your hat and coat off.

Philomena I'll keep it on, me hair going thin.

Queen Mother And mine.

They pat their hair.

Philomena You don't remember me?

Queen Mother We've met before?

Philomena In Jamaica. I was wearing a red dress and waving a little flag. The heighth of June.

Queen Mother Now what year would that be? A Caribbean Tour. 1927?

Philomena Yes! You *do* remember me.

Queen Mother The public were adorable in 1927.

Philomena Well they gone downhill since then. In 1927 you could take your door off its hinges, show the world what you got. Now you got the poor stealin' from the poor.

Queen Mother I've never lived on my own. I'm frightened.

Philomena I got *three* chains on *my* door. I want to die peaceful, look nice in my coffin.

Queen Mother Mrs Toussaint, I need a companion to sit with me in the evening. I can't afford to pay you a wage, but you could share my gas fire.

Philomena OK, but I got conditions. No drinking, no betting, no blasphemy, and no drug-taking, not while I'm in the house.

Queen Mother I agree to those conditions. Thank you.

Philomena *looks at the album.*

Philomena Who's that bag o' bones?

Queen Mother (*viciously*) Wallace Simpson. I'll never forgive her. I'd always thought of myself as a nice woman until I met her.

Philomena Calm yourself, woman, I'll make you a drink.

Queen Mother Yes, I usually have a drink at this time.

Philomena And that is my Aunt Mathilda. Evil woman. Drank herself to death. You want tea or coffee?

Philomena *goes into the kitchen. The* **Queen Mother** *takes a gin bottle out of her handbag, has a nip of gin and starts to read the 'Sporting Life'.*

Queen Mother (*shouting*) You'll find some Earl Grey in the cupboard. (*Pause.*) I will never forgive her for seducing David and making him abdicate. He knew my husband didn't want to be King.

Philomena (*off*) I can't find that Earl Grey nonsense. You'll have to have tea!

Queen Mother Poor George suffered terribly with his nerves.

Fitzroy *comes in.*

Fitzroy Anybody there?

The **Queen Mother** *is shocked. She holds her bag out.*

Queen Mother Take it! Take it!

Fitzroy No, you keep it. I'm an insolvency accountant. Business is booming. I'm Fitzroy. Is my Mum here?

Queen Mother She's in the kitchen.

Fitzroy *pulls a 'Sporting Life' out of his pocket.*

Fitzroy Snap! You like the gee-gees then?

Queen Mother Yes. Do you know form?

Fitzroy Yeah, yeah, but keep it quiet.

Queen Mother Who trained my grandson's horse, Sea Swell?

Fitzroy Nick Gaselee. Duke of Gloucester Memorial Trophy. By two lengths: six to one. Do you fancy a flutter?

He looks towards the kitchen.

Queen Mother (*giving him a fiver*) Purple Prince, Kempton Park, 4.30.

Fitzroy To win?

Queen Mother Oh yes, the going's soft, he likes that!

Fitzroy I'll say hello to her then I'll phone it through, I got a phone in the car.

Queen Mother Did you know your mother goes to bed at five o'clock to keep warm?

Fitzroy I give her money every week but she don't spend it. She reckons they gonna stop paying her pension.

Fitzroy *goes into the kitchen.*

Fitzroy (*off*) Hello Mum. Hob-nobbing with royalty now eh?

Philomena (*off*) Fitzroy! You lookin' thin boy. Do you want a cup of tea? The kettle nearly boiled.

Fitzroy (*off*) Yeah. I just gotta go out to the car though Mum.

Philomena (*off*) No. You help me find the china, nothing's unpacked.

Fitzroy (*off*) OK, Mum.

Diana *rushes into the living room.*

Diana Granny, you couldn't do me a ginormous favour, could you? I'm sort of desperate.

Queen Mother *Another* favour, Diana?

Diana I know. William's going to a Heritage Centre with the school tomorrow.

Queen Mother Lovely! (*Pause.*) What is a Heritage Centre?

Diana It's something to do with British industry. It's for history.

Philomena *comes in with the tea.*

Philomena Hello Mrs Lady Diana. Did you see me boy's car parked outside?

Diana The Merc? That's your son's is it?

Philomena Him work hard for it. Here Mrs Queen Mother. By the look of your teeth you take sugar. (*To* **Diana**.) You want one?

Diana That would be lovely.

Philomena Fitzroy, find the sugar bowl.

Philomena *goes out.*

Fitzroy (*off*) It must be in the other box.

Diana He needs two pounds to pay for the coach. I've tried everybody else.

Queen Mother I'm sorry Diana, I've just placed . . . *spent* my last five pounds.

Philomena (*off*) Mrs Queen Mother!

Queen Mother Yes, Philomena!

Philomena Show Mrs Lady Diana the photograph of me boys when they was children.

Diana *looks at the photograph.*

Diana (*shouting*) They're really, really sweet Mrs Toussaint!

Philomena (*off*) Yes. They good-looking boys.

Queen Mother I had a crush on Paul Robeson once, such a big handsome man. Lovely manners too, for a communist.

Fitzroy *comes in.*

Diana Oh hello, I'm . . .

Fitzroy I know who you are. *You* are the most beautiful woman in the world.

Diana No, I look dreadful. I've been decorating . . . these clothes . . . Lovely Merc.

Fitzroy Yeah. It *is* a bit special.

Diana Do you live round here?

Fitzroy No! I've got a two-bedroomed Tudor townhouse near the motorway.

Diana Great!

The **Queen Mother** *looks at her watch.*

Queen Mother (*to* **Fitzroy**) They're *off* I think.

Fitzroy *and* **Diana** *are gazing at each other.*

Fitzroy It's got an integral garage.

Diana Fabuloso.

Queen Mother Purple Prince!

Fitzroy Yeah. Back in a minute, Princess.

Fitzroy *goes off.*

Philomena (*off*) *Now* where that boy gone? He in an' out like the tide at Blackpool.

Queen Mother How's Charles?

Diana I dunno. I haven't seen him. He's doing boring things to his garden. Fertilising his maypole, or something.

Queen Mother And William?

Diana Wills is really, really happy. He's got some friends. They're quite sweet. Well, perhaps not *sweet.*

Pause.

Do you think Mrs Toussaint could spare some cash?

Philomena *comes in.*

Philomena The answer is no! I'm saving all me money up for me old age.

Philomena *goes out.*

Diana I wonder if Margot's in?

Queen Mother She's usually at home at this time. She seems to be very popular lately. Surprising isn't it? Considering how unpleasant she is.

Diana Thank God Wills gets free school meals, otherwise he'd go without lunch.

Queen Mother I'd go hungry without my Wheels on Meals.

Diana I think you'll find the phrase is Meals on Wheels, Granny.

Fitzroy *comes in.*

Fitzroy (*to* **Queen Mother**) Purple Prince did us proud. Twelve to one. Not bad eh? I'll drop in tomorrow shall I? With the £60.

Queen Mother Splendid! Please do.

Fitzroy Nice to meet you both!

Diana I'm going myself actually.

Fitzroy Can I drop you anywhere.

Diana I'm only going fifty yards.

Fitzroy Fifty yards of heaven. Bye, Mum.

Fitzroy *exits.*

Philomena (*off*) Bye bye, Fitzroy.

Diana Bye, Granny.

They go out.

Queen Mother (*shouting*) A nice young man, Philomena!

Philomena (*off*) It's time the boy was married. But him too choosy.

Queen Mother The reason we're all here now is that we weren't choosy *enough* when it came to finding Charles a wife.

Philomena It weren't your fault. Virgins are thin on the ground in Hell Close too.

Queen Mother You and Fitzroy are amazingly alike.

Philomena You think so? No, Fitzroy takes after his father.

Queen Mother No, you're two peas in a pod. I'd like to see you two together, side by side.

Philomena No, it haint possible. He too busy. The boy split himself in half as it is.

Scene Seven

The Queen's kitchen

The **Queen** *is doing the washing up.* **Prince Philip** *is wearing his dressing-gown and pyjamas.*

Queen You haven't shaved Philip, and it's nearly four o'clock.

Philip I'm growing a beard. What are you doing to those plates?

Queen I'm doing the washing-up.

Philip You don't seem to be getting many bubbles.

Queen No, I can't understand it. Diana said Ajax was wonderful stuff. You haven't washed, either.

Philip Bathroom's too bloody cold.

Queen You've been wearing your pyjamas and dressing-gown for three days.

Philip I don't intend to go out. Why bother to change?

Queen But you must go out.

Philip Why?

Queen For fresh air, exercise.

Philip There is no fresh air in Hell-bloody-Close. It stinks. It's ugly. I shall stay in-bloody-doors until the day I die.

Sound off: knocking on the front door.

The **Queen** *goes off.*

Philip Don't answer it. We're forced to live with them, but it doesn't mean we have to speak to them.

Trish (*off*) Mrs Windsor? I'm Trish McPherson.

Trish *comes in followed by the* **Queen**.

Trish . . . from the 'Back to Basics' Centre. A leftover from the Major years. We're changing it to the Family Help Centre as soon as we've used the stationery up.

Trish *takes* **Philip**'*s hand, and shakes it.*

Trish Mr Windsor.

Philip Mountbatten's the name!

Trish *looks around.*

Trish . . . Well, it's cosy isn't it?

Queen It won't be for long, the gas is due to go at any moment. Do sit down.

Trish Well, don't worry about me being cold. I'm dressed from head to toe in yak's wool. Do you know Tibet at all?

Queen Yes, I've dined with the Dalai Lama several times.

Trish Of course! I keep forgetting! You look like such an ordinary woman, here, in this setting. I must admit I was a bit nervous, about meeting you. I mean how do you talk to somebody whose head you're used to licking and sticking on an envelope?

Queen You seem to have overcome your reserve quite easily, Miss McPherson.

Trish So, how are you coping?

Queen Quite well, money's a problem.

Trish In what way?

Queen I seem to have spent it all.

Trish But are you integrating into the community? Getting to know your neighbours?

Queen Certainly, I've borrowed money from most of them.

Trish Forgive me but you seem to be a little bit obsessed with money.

Queen (*heatedly*) It's because I haven't got any! Our pension book, though promised, has yet to arrive. The fifty pounds each we were given simply disappeared.

Philip Vanished. Light bulbs, television licence.

Queen Dog food. Gas, electricity, something called Brillo pads which Diana said were absolutely essential.

Philip We could have done without a TV licence. Nobody else round here has one.

Queen Philip. I was, until a few days ago, the nominal head of our British legal system. Without a TV licence I could not have allowed myself to watch TV.

Philip She wasted more money on a couple of hot water bottles . . .

Queen (*to* **Trish**) We needed them. The first time I awoke in this house it was so cold. I looked across at Philip and thought he was exuding ectoplasm from his mouth.

Trish I'm afraid you're in the same position as a lot of working-class people in this country.

Philip Working class! They don't work! Can't even clean up their gardens! Wouldn't take 'em half a bloody hour.

Trish I'm afraid your own garden is a potential health hazard, Mr Windsor.

Queen I've been asking him to clean it up for three days.

Philip (*very angry*) I don't want to go outside!

Queen Darling, go upstairs and put some clothes on.

William *comes in carrying* **Harris**.

William Ay up our grandma. Ay up our grandad. Y'oright?

Queen (*laughing*) William that's a frightfully good impersonation of the local dialect.

William It ain't an impersonation. If I talk posh I get my cowin' face smashed in!

Queen Harris, you've got blood on your nose!

Harris *growls*.

William 'Es bin in a fight on the reccy. 'E started it. I seen 'im. I were with me posse.

Diana *runs in.*

Diana William! Give it back to me! That was my last pound!

William I ain't 'ad it!

Diana You know Daddy hasn't paid me a penny yet. Please, give it back to me, darling.

William I ain't 'ad yer poxy pound!

Queen Don't talk to your mother like that, William. . . .

Harris *barks.*

Queen . . . And take him out and shut him in the coal shed! Wicked boy! Wicked!

Exit **William** *with* **Harris**. **Harris** *barks.*

Diana He is a wicked boy. He took it out of my bag.

Queen I was talking to Harris. I'm sure William would never steal from you.

Diana But he did!

William *returns, with* **Harris**.

William 'Arris 'as bit me faxin' finger!

William *rushes off again, with* **Harris**.

Queen William! Must you talk like that? Diana, will you speak to that boy!

Diana I can't cope with him, he's turning into a thug.

Philip (*groans*) Lilibet, I've had a-bloody-nuff of this. I'm going back to bed. Please bring me a cup of Lapsang Souchong.

Philip *goes upstairs.*

Queen Of course darling, but they don't have Lapsang Souchong at Kwiksave. It'll have to be PG Tips.

Diana I know he took it! I had two pounds thirty-nine in my bag this morning. I bought two beefburger things from Penguin's Palace, so that left one pound and nine. I went into the garden to unblock the drain and when I came back all I had was nine pence.

Queen My grandson is *not* a thief.

Diana Yes, but my son is! How do other people manage? I was up half the night drying William's school trousers in the gas oven.

Philip *returns*.

Philip Surprised you didn't put your head in it. You've tried everything else to do yourself in.

Diana I *fell* down those stairs! I did *not* throw myself down them!

Philip And I'd like the tea in my World Wildlife mug please.

Philip *goes back upstairs*.

Diana You couldn't lend me a pound for a pair of tights could you, Your Majesty?

Queen Diana, I have absolutely no money at all. I don't know how we will survive the weekend.

Trish There's plenty going on at the Community Centre. You must all take advantage of the facilities.

Diana Facilities! There's a bouncer on the door of the Community Centre! The church roof is covered in razor wire, and it isn't possible to window shop as there aren't any faxing windows.

Diana *exits*.

Trish May I suggest you fill in these forms Mrs Windsor. They're quite simple. Under special circumstances you can get an emergency payment from the DSS office in town. But you'll have to hurry, they close at 5.30. I'll let myself out, shall I?

Trish *exits*.

Queen 'Entitlement to Council Tax benefit is calculated in respect of a benefit stroke Council Tax benefit week: a period of seven days beginning on a Monday. So your Council Tax is converted into a weekly figure. An annual personal community charge is divided by 365 or 366 and multiplied by seven.' Oh God! 'Similarly if a collective Council Tax charge contribution is payable other than weekly, a weekly figure is obtained by dividing the figure by the number of days . . .' What? This is impossible! 'And multiplying by seven.' It could be written in Swahili. Oh Crawfie, I'm lost. I don't understand it. I can't do it.

The ghost of **Crawfie** *appears*.

Crawfie Come on, my little princess. Head up, shoulders back. Pick up your pencil and write down your weekly income.

The **Queen** *writes*.

Crawfie Good, good, now eighty per cent of your maximum benefit.

Queen I don't know what that is, Crawfie.

Crawfie I'll tell you just this once. In your case it's eight pounds. Now what's eighty per cent of eight pounds?

Queen I don't know.

Crawfie I taught you percentages when you were ten years old. Eighty per cent of eight pounds, princess.

Queen Is it six pounds twenty?

Crawfie No, look you forgot to carry the two.

Queen Oh yes. It's six pounds *forty*.

Crawfie Good girl. Now take that away from that. Find what they call the applicable amount, and write it all out neatly on the form.

The **Queen** *fills in the form.*

Queen I was awfully sad when you died, Crawfie. I missed you terribly.

Crawfie I've missed you. You were always my favourite. So serious.

Queen I've let you down.

Crawfie No. (*Pause.*) My poor little princess. Do you still leave your bed three times a night to check that your shoes are straight?

Queen Only sometimes. I've finished.

The **Queen** *shows the form to* **Crawfie**.

Crawfie You've signed it Elizabeth R. Cross it out.

The **Queen** *writes.*

Crawfie You'll have to hurry, they close at half-past five, and I'm sure they don't open again until Monday.

The **Queen** *and* **Crawfie** *embrace.*

Queen We lived in paradise, Crawfie.

Scene Eight

Hell Close

Prince Charles *is walking along wearing wellingtons and a cap. He is carrying a spade over his shoulder.*

Leanne *approaches in the opposite direction. She is pushing* **Clinton**
in a pushchair.

Charles Good evening, Leanne. (*He tips his cap.*)

Leanne Hiya, bin diggin'?

Charles Er . . . Yes . . . I'm rather dirty, I'm afraid.

Leanne I don't mind a bit of dirt.

Charles No, nor I. It's some time since I got . . . dirty. Got
down to it. Felt the earth . . . er . . . move.

Leanne Do you know owt about bushes?

Charles What kind of bush?

Leanne Just a bush, my bush. Only it's got out of control.

Charles Has it? Has it? Then it will need cutting back.

Leanne Do you reckon you could cut my bush back?

Charles Er . . . most certainly. I must confess, I'm the sort
of chap who enjoys a vigorous pruning. Will your bush be
. . . er . . . in tomorrow morning?

Leanne I'll make sure it is.

Charles Tomorrow.

He tips his cap.

They part.

Scene Nine

DSS office

Amanda Boniface *sits behind her counter trying to process*
Leanne's claim. **Clinton** *is over* **Leanne***'s shoulder, whining.* **Mrs**
Newman *is standing meekly at the counter anxious to be seen. The*

Queen *comes in with* **Harris** *in her arms. She stands behind* **Mrs Newman**.

Harris *is growling.*

Queen I know darling boy, you're hungry aren't you?

Amanda (*to* **Leanne**) But you're not *on* the computer.

Leanne Course I'm on the computer! It keeps spelling me name wrong!

Clinton *fidgets.*

Harris *growls.*

Leanne Don't start Clinton! (*To* **Amanda**.) Grubbe. Two B's and an E.

Amanda Just a moment.

A drunken **Scotsman** *enters, lurching around.*

Queen Twenty-five past five and I need money for gas and electricity and food . . .

Scotsman (*pushing in*) I havnae got a number, but just tell me this, lassie . . .

Amanda You won't be seen without a number.

Scotsman I just want to ask you a question, see . . .

Mrs Newman (*timidly*) You're pushing in.

Scotsman No. No. I just want to ask . . .

Queen (*to* **Scotsman**) Please stand behind me!

Scotsman I only want to ask . . .

Queen But you're wasting time, they close in four minutes and there's somebody in front of me. I must be seen!

Clinton *cries.* **Harris** *barks.*

Leanne (*shouting at* **Amanda**) All 'e's 'ad is a packet of crisps today! He's 'ungry!

Queen I'm hungry. It's a horrid feeling. It makes one want to growl and snap one's teeth

Mrs Newman *bursts into tears.*

Amanda (*to* **Leanne**) Are you Leanne Grubbe? 15 Hellebore Close?

Leanne Yes!

Amanda Your giro was processed nine days ago.

Leanne But it's not come!

Queen (*to* **Mrs Newman**) Three minutes before they close the doors!

Mrs Newman (*to* **Queen**) It's my lad. He's took me money for drugs! I'm sitting in the dark at home. (*She sobs.*)

Clinton *cries.* **Harris** *barks.*

Queen Stop it! Stop it!

The **Queen** *hits* **Harris** *hard. He yelps.*

Amanda (*to* **Leanne**) I'll give you ten pounds. If your giro's not come by Monday, ring up.

Leanne Why? Nobody ever answers the faxin' phone!

Queen (*shouting*) Will you please hurry!

Mrs Newman (*sobbing*) What am I going to do?

The **Queen** *looks at her watch.*

Scotsman (*to* **Queen**) Hey, don't I know you hen? Your face is awful familiar. Do you drink in the Prince of Wales near the bus station? Is your name Queenie?

Queen No, that is not my name.

Scotsman It'll come to me, dinna worry. I nivver forget a face. What's the hold up eh! I fought for my Queen!

He takes his hat off and sings. **Harris** *barks.*

. . . God save our gracious Queen, Long live our noble Queen, God save our Queen.

The **Scotsman** *tries to comfort* **Mrs Newman**. *He offers her a drink. She takes it.*

Amanda *gives* **Leanne** *ten pounds*. **Leanne** *shows it to* **Clinton**.

Leanne (*delighted*) Look what Mam's got! Ten pounds! I'll get you some chips on the way 'ome and a packet of nappies an' we'll have the fire on in the front room.

Amanda *stands and puts her coat on, puts her bag over her shoulder.*

Harris *sniffs at* **Clinton** *and growls.* **Leanne** *exits.*

Mrs Newman *goes up to the counter.*

Amanda Mrs Newman I told you this morning. The DSS can't subsidise your son's drug habit.

Mrs Newman But I'm sitting in the dark. What shall I do?

Queen (*to* **Amanda**) You can't go! I need an emergency payment. I demand that you work until exactly half-past five! I command it!

Amanda *sits down reluctantly.*

Scotsman You tell her hen, you tell her.

The **Queen** *goes up to* **Amanda** *at the counter. Their conversation is conducted at great speed.*

Amanda Why do you need an emergency payment?

Queen Because I'm penniless. My pension book hasn't arrived.

Scotsman I fought for my Queen.

Mrs Newman What am I going to do?

Amanda Name?

Queen Elizabeth Windsor.

Amanda Address?

Queen 45 Hellebore Close. Saffron Lane Estate.

Scotsman Falklands. Bluff Cove.

Amanda How long have you lived there?

Queen Four days.

Mrs Newman I'm in the dark.

Exits.

Amanda Previous address?

Queen Buckingham Palace, The Mall, London.

Amanda *gives the* **Queen** *a beady look.*

Amanda And what were you doing there?

Queen I was being the Queen.

Amanda Have you just left an Institution?

Queen Yes, I suppose I have.

Amanda Then I'm not authorised to make you an emergency payment.

Queen Miss Boniface. That badge you're wearing. Is it the Canine Defence League?

Amanda Yes it is, my mother breeds Jack Russells. Goodnight.

Queen (*to* **Harris**) Die Harris! Die!

Harris *goes limp, his tongue lolls out of his mouth.*

Queen Miss Boniface, will you help my dog, Harris? He hasn't eaten for three days.

Harris *coughs.*

Amanda Poor thing! You shouldn't keep a dog if you can't look after it properly. I suppose he was a Christmas present.

Queen Yes, he was!

Amanda *opens drawer and gives the* **Queen** *a £5 note.*

Amanda Here! Make sure you spend it on dog food and a packet of Bob Martins. He's in terrible condition.

Exits.

Harris *looks up at the* **Queen** *and grins. They start to walk out.*

Scotsman (*to* **Queen**) I know who you look like. That woman who looks like the Queen. You shid cash in on it. You shid, you shid go on telly and impersonate Jeanette Charles. You shid!

Harris *growls.*

Scotsman Fax off, you nasty wee dog. (*To* **Queen**.) You shid! You shid!

Queen *exits, followed by* **Scotsman**.

Scene Ten

Hell Close. Night.

Margaret *is standing in Hell Close smoking a cigarette.* **Inspector Holyland** *walks by on patrol.*

Holyland Hello Your Royal Highness. Lovely evening, isn't it?

Margaret I wouldn't know, I haven't got my glasses on. Have you seen Ludlow?

Holyland He's involved in rather an unpleasant domestic at the moment. Can I help you?

Margaret No. It's about a case *he's* investigating. The art theft.

Holyland Right. Yes, I leave the art crime to Ludlow. We seem to be having a spate of 'em lately. A Mr Blobby poster was snatched from a toddler's fingers only last week. Goodnight Your Royal Highness.

Holyland *strolls off.*

Queen *enters.*

The **Queen** *and* **Margaret** *pass in the street.*

Queen Hello, Bud.

Margaret You look ghastly, Lilibet.

Queen So would you if you'd just come from the Social.

Margaret The Social! How quickly you have assimilated the language of the poor.

Queen It's desperate. One could be in a third world country during a drought. People will do *anything* to get hold of some ready cash.

Margaret They will? I can't be poor. I shall have to find a way to increase my income.

Queen I shall have to get a part-time job.

Margaret Doing what?

Queen I don't know, one's skills are somewhat redundant around here. The next thing I'm due to open is a tin of dog food.

Harris *barks.*

Queen I must get him home. He's hungry, (*To* **Harris.**) aren't you darling? Night, Bud.

Margaret Goodnight, Lilibet.

Queen *exits as* **Diana** *enters.*

Diana Margot! . . . I didn't want to ask you in front of her but could you lend me five pounds? I need something for the weekend.

Margaret Really, Diana! You sound like an old-fashioned barber. . . . This is the second time since we've got here. I ought to start charging you interest. (*Pause.*) In fact I shall. I will give you five pounds and you must repay me seven.

Diana But I'm family!

Margaret Family! It was family that lost me the love of my life. I set no great store by family.

Diana But that means you make a profit of two pounds for doing absolutely nothing.

Margaret It's called commerce Diana. It makes the world go round. And given your suicidal tendencies, I judge yours to be a high risk loan.

Diana For the last time. I did not jump down those bloody stairs!

Leanne *enters, pushing* **Clinton**.

Diana When do I have to pay you back?

Margaret Within seven days. After that I shall charge you interest at twenty-five per cent a day.

Diana And when I've paid you back I shall get a proper loan from a bank!

Diana *starts to leave and* **Leanne** *laughs.*

Leanne (*to* **Diana**) A bank! They'll show you the door as soon as they hear your address.

Diana *exits.*

Leanne (*to* **Margaret**) So, you lend money do you?

Margaret I do have a soft heart. But to whom am I speaking?

Leanne Leanne, Leanne Grubbe, two B's and an E.

Margaret Miss or Mrs?

Leanne Mrs but he's run off, to Wales.

Margaret Wales! Dreadful place, rain and socialists.

Leanne Thing is I need twenty-four pound by tomorrer else I get the water cut off.

Margaret Do you own anything of value?

Leanne Only me family benefit book.

She gives it to **Margaret** *who flicks through the pages.*

Leanne I can't have no water, not with Christmas coming.

Margaret I'll give you twenty-four pounds in exchange for your book.

Leanne But there's forty-two pounds in that!

Margaret I have to cover my expenses. And I cannot possibly live on the pension I receive from the State.

Leanne Our Mam does.

Margaret But your Mam is one of those whiskery shapeless old hags one encounters at the Post Office isn't she?

Leanne Sounds like our Mam, yeah.

Margaret And I suppose when she dies you'll jump into her grave won't you, unless restrained by relatives?

Leanne Yeah. They 'ad to 'old me back at me Grandad's grave.

Margaret *counts out twenty-four pounds into* **Leanne***'s hand.*

Margaret You people don't have blood in your veins, you have sentiment. I have no intention of looking like your Mam.

Ludlow *comes on.*

Ludlow How's it going, Leanne?

Leanne How do you think! You're late, we won't have time now. He'll be awake soon.

Ludlow There was an accident. A moped went off the road. It had to swerve to avoid a corgi.

Margaret Was the corgi killed?

Ludlow No.

Margaret Pity.

Leanne Don't bother comin' round in the morning. I'm havin' some gardening done.

Leanne *goes.*

Margaret Constable I'd like to talk to you about art.

Ludlow I'd like nothing better, Your Royal Highness. But I've got to go home now. It's Wendy's birthday.

Margaret You've bought her a present have you?

Ludlow No, not yet. I'm going to get her a sink tidy on the way home.

Margaret A sink tidy! You wouldn't prefer to give her a Titian? A sublime work of genius for . . . how much do you have on you?

Ludlow Seventeen pound sixty-nine pence.

Margaret For seventeen pounds sixty-nine pence.

Ludlow She really wanted a sink tidy . . . but I'll get her one for Christmas. Shall I pick it up now?

Margaret Give me five minutes. I have to pick up something to save my life.

Ludlow From the late night chemist?

Margaret No, from the late night off-licence. Adieu.

Leanne (*off*) Ludlow I didn't mean it. Come and see me!

Margaret You seem to be remarkably popular for an officer of the law.

Margaret *goes.*

Ludlow I think I went a bit far with the community policing. Got a bit too involved. I like women, that's my problem. Seems that every time I go into a house, a crying woman throws herself into my arms. It started with Leanne. Her husband Malcolm threw her down the stairs. She's only a little thing. He's built like King Kong. It took three of us and a dog to get him in the van. Violet was the next. Her second husband beat her up so bad her face looked like a gorgonzola cheese. I had to give her some comfort. Before I knew it I was catching me toe nails on her nylon sheets.

Diana *appears at top of stairs.*

Diana (*calls*) Ludlow! Ludlow! I'm so worried. Have you seen William? He hasn't come home.

Ludlow It's got to stop! I'm a married man now. It's only five weeks since I stood at the altar in my top hat and tails! Actually, that's when I first started to go off Wendy. She lifted her veil and smiled at me and I saw that she had a cornflake stuck to her front teeth. (*Pause.*) It was in the shape of Australia. (*Pause.*) Diana would never allow that to happen. She's not mortal, she's a goddess and they don't eat cornflakes. They live on adoration and ambrosia and I'm not talking about rice pudding.

Ludlow *exits.*

Scene Eleven

Inside Diana's house

Diana *dials on a portable phone.*

Diana Sarah? It's me! (*Pause.*) Diana! (*Pause.*) Diana.
(*Pause.*) Your sister Diana. I left my number on your answer
phone thingy, why didn't you call me back? (*Pause.*) You
can't be as busy as I am. I have to do everything. Sarah, I
hope you're not going to be snooty because I've sort of gone
down in the world. (*Pause.*) It's worse for me! I look like a
dog, I do! You should see my nails. I had my hands down a
drain this morning. (*Pause.*) No, the people are really, really
sweet. One in particular. (*Pause.*) Fitzroy. (*Pause.*) A
Mercedes. Sares, you couldn't do me a favour, could you?
Send me something to wear? Tart style if poss. A Wonderbra
would be fabuloso. They're really big on cleavage round
here. I shall have to go, Sares, Nelly the elephant's here.

Charles *enters.*

Charles Where did you get that phone?

Diana Ludlow gave it to me. It's for crime prevention.

Charles Is William inside?

Diana No, he's out somewhere.

Charles He knows it's my access day. We were going to put
the bean sticks up.

Diana Did you get a letter from Harry?

Charles Yes, sweet.

Diana So *sweet.*

Charles He can't spell.

Diana It doesn't matter.

Charles I must confess Diana, that I'm the sort of person
who thinks that it *does* matter . . . profoundly.

William Ay up our dad. Sorry I'm late, only I were wi' me posse.

Charles William please! You don't have to keep up this ridiculous linguistic charade with your own family.

William 'Ave ya brought our Mam 'er money?

Charles No, I'm paying it to the Child Protection Agency now.

William That's faxin' stupid. You should give it to our Mam, in 'er 'and. What a *Dumbo*!

Charles *attempts to smack* **William** *around the head.* **Diana** *protects* **William**.

Charles Don't call me Dumbo.

William If you hit me I'll get the Social onto you.

Diana Don't you dare to lay a finger on this poor little boy! You bully! You adulterer! You liar!

Charles I was forced into adultery! Making love to you was like jigging about on a mortuary slab!

Diana Get away from my house! Get away!

Diana *pushes* **Charles** *out of the house.*

The **Queen** *is at her front door.*

Violet *is at her front door. She is holding* **Clinton** *and laughing with* **Leanne**.

Philomena *and the* **Queen Mother** *are walking arm in arm, on the way to Church. They are carrying hymn books.*
Wilf *is pushing his battery along in a pushchair.*

Queen Harris! Harris!

Charles, **Diana** *and* **William** *run into the street arguing.*

William Leave our Mam alone!

Violet Ay up! Trouble!

Diana (*crying*) Other men find me desirable!

Violet *passes* **Clinton** *to* **Leanne** *who puts him in his pushchair.*

Wilf Me for one.

Violet (*to* **Wilf**) Eh! Keep your nose out!

Charles Come on William!

Charles *pulls on* **William**'s *left arm.* **Diana** *pulls on the right.*

Diana He's staying with me!

Charles No. He's coming with me! It's my access day.

Queen Charles! Diana! Go inside at once!

Charles (*roaring*) Don't tell me what to do Mummy! I'm a grown man!

Diana (*to* **Queen**) Why don't you just stay out of it?

Queen Mother Why is everybody being so horrid?

Queen Diana! Don't you dare speak to me like that.

William (*to* **Charles**) Let go of me!

Diana You're hurting him Charles!

William *struggles free and runs off.*

William I'm goin' to me posse!

Diana Wills! Wills!

Much of the following dialogue overlaps.

Charles That boy has become a delinquent!

Diana And it's all your fault! You were never there!

Charles (*to* **Diana**) I couldn't bloody well stand being there.

Leanne (*to* **Diana**) Because you were bloody well frigid, that's why.

Charles (*to* **Leanne**) Just be quiet, woman!

Wilf (*to* **Queen**) I said your family'd be trouble!

Violet (*to* **Wilf**) And I said keep your nose out, Wilf!

Queen (*to* **Wilf**) Mr Toby, we've never given you a moment's trouble!

Diana (*to* **Charles**) We all know where you were! The whole of Britain knows where you were. Tampax Head!

Philomena It's a shame on the Sabbath day.

Wilf (*to* **Queen**) Your 'usband gev us trouble shoutin' and carryin' on. The walls are thin in these houses, you know!

Queen (*to* **Wilf**) The walls certainly *are* thin! I can hear *you* farting in bed.

Queen Mother Elizabeth, *do* stop them shouting!

Charles (*to* **Diana**) Don't bloody bring all that up again!

Violet (*to* **Wilf**) Gerrin. Now!

Violet *grabs* **Wilf** *and bundles him towards her front door and inside the house.*

Queen Mother Elizabeth! Don't be so vulgar! You mustn't shout in the street!

Queen Why not? Everybody else does.

Philomena (*shouting*) The Lord's looking down on you all and he hain't too pleased! (*To* **Queen Mother**.) You comin' to church?

Leanne (*to* **Charles**) I say it's her fault, she's just a faxin' tease.

Violet (*to* **Leanne**) Stop stirring it up, Leanne.

Queen Mother (*to* **Philomena**) You go on dear, I'm needed here.

Philomena *walks off.*

Queen Everybody else can shout and scream when they please, I've never screamed, not once.

Queen Mother I'm ashamed of you, Elizabeth.

Leanne (*to* **Charles**, *about* **Diana**) What I wanna know is, 'ow she got a clothing grant from the DSS. Nobody else has 'ad one round 'ere.

Queen (*to* **Leanne**) What are you implying?

Leanne Dorkin's always round 'er house. . . .

Violet Shut your faxin' gob, Leanne. Before I shove me fist down it.

Leanne . . . An' that Fitzroy Toussaint, an' Ludlow.

Violet You can't talk. You've had more men in you than Wembley Stadium on Cup Final Day.

Charles (*to* **Diana**, *referring to* **Leanne**'s *accusation.*) Is this true?

Diana They're friends.

Mrs Newman *enters.*

Mrs Newman What's going on?

Everyone ignores **Mrs Newman**.

Leanne (*to* **Violet**) Think you're sommat special, don't you, 'cos you're friends with the Queen?

Violet (*to* **Leanne**) I told you to faxin' shut it!

Leanne Mek me! Go on, mek me!

Violet *lunges at* **Leanne**.

Philip (*from window*) I'm trying to go quietly mad in here. Show some consideration.

Philip *retreats.*

Charles (*to* **Diana**) If you're having men around the house, I'm not paying you another penny!

Diana Then I'll never give you a divorce!

Leanne *is screaming, being ragged about by* **Violet**. *The* **Queen Mother** *is attempting to part them.*

Violet (*to* **Leanne**) Ludlow told me you were crap at it!

Leanne (*to* **Violet**) Ludlow told me you were faxin' past it!

Queen Mother Stop it! Stop it! I'll throw a bucket of water over you.

Mrs Newman (*to* **Diana**) That's right, me duck. Stand up for yourself.

Queen (*to* **Queen Mother**) Mummy, come out of the way! (*To* **Violet**.) Violet! Please! (*Looking for the dog.*) Harris, darling!

Violet *has got* **Leanne** *on the floor.*

Philip *appears at window again.*

Philip I shall throw myself off the bloody roof!

Philip *retreats.*

Fitzroy *enters.*

Fitzroy What's going on?

Queen (*calling up to the window*) Philip, Philip, is Harris in the house?

Diana (*to* **Fitzroy**) Oh, Fitz. He's been foul to me!

Queen (*calling to* **Philip**) Have you seen Harris?

Leanne (*to* **Violet**) You ain't the only one to be friends wi' Royalty! Is she, Charles?

Charles (*to* **Leanne**) Shut your mouth, you silly tart!

Diana What's going on, Charles?

Violet (*to* **Leanne**) You been shaggin' 'im an' all?

Queen Mother You're all being so vulgar!

Leanne (*to* **Charles**) I weren't a silly tart last night, were I? I were 'Darling Leanne'. . . .

Fitzroy Thank God I got the hell out of here!

Leanne (*continuing to* **Charles**) . . . You told me you loved me!

Diana He doesn't know the meaning of the word. . . . King Clinton!

Queen Oh my God!

Mrs Newman What are we going to *do*?

Wilf *appears at his upstairs window.*

Wilf (*shouting*) Violet! When we 'avin' us dinner?

Violet It'll be late! I've got me 'ands full!

Charles (*to* **Fitzroy**) She's only after your Mercedes.

Fitzroy My *wrecked* Mercedes. . . .

Charles Serves you right. You jumped-up yuppy.

Fitzroy (*continuing*) . . . Your lad was with the gang that wrecked my car.

Diana Well Fitz, we don't know that.

Holyland (*entering*) Break it up. . . .

Fitzroy (*to* **Charles**) Listen. I worked for my money.

Holyland (*continuing*) . . . Come on, break it up.

Charles (*to* **Fitzroy**) You try being a bloody Prince twenty-four hours a day.

Diana He's more a man than you, Charles.

Holyland Go back to your homes.

Queen Mother Elizabeth, why don't you *do* something?!

Queen Why don't *you* do something for once. . . .

Holyland Leanne! Violet! Break it up!

Queen (*continuing, to* **Queen Mother**) . . . *I'm* looking for my dog.

Leanne (*to* **Holyland** *about* **Violet**) She started it!

Violet And I'll finish it an' all, you toe rag!

Holyland *grabs* **Violet** *by the arm.*

Violet Let go! You're breaking my faxin' arm.

Leanne Charlie, Charlie! Get him off me!

Queen Mother (*hitting* **Holyland**) Don't hurt Mrs Toby. She's taking me to the pantomime on Tuesday.

Mrs Newman (*appealing to everyone*) What are we going to do?

Mrs Newman *hovers over* **Violet** *and* **Leanne**.

Queen Mother We must separate them.

The **Queen**, *the* **Queen Mother** *and* **Mrs Newman** *try to part* **Violet** *and* **Leanne**.

Fitzroy (*to* **Charles**) He were with those lads that wrecked my car. I read books for that car. . . .

Charles (*unconcerned*) It's insured, isn't it?

Fitzroy (*continuing, to* **Charles**) . . . Passed exams.

Queen My dog! He's a pure-bred Pembrokeshire Corgi!

Fitzroy (*to* **Charles**) You live in a moral vacuum! I've got to blame the parents.

Diana You don't mean that, do you Fitz?

The **Queen Mother** *hits* **Holyland** *again.*

Queen Mother Take that, you horrid man!

Holyland Do that again, madam, and you'll be waving through the bars . . .

Leanne Charlie! Charlie! Be a man!

Holyland (*continuing his speech to the* **Queen Mother**) . . . of a prison cell.

Queen (*still speaking of her dog*) He's never been out all night.

Holyland *attempts to push the* **Queen Mother** *out of the way. She stumbles and is caught by* **Fitzroy**. **Charles** *jumps on* **Holyland**'s *back.*

Charles You fascist pig!

Queen Harris.

Holyland *wrestles* **Charles** *to the ground.*

Holyland (*to* **Charles**) You're under arrest for assaulting a Police Officer, and for calling me a fascist!

Queen (*to* **Holyland**) You're a policeman. Help me find my dog.

Everyone looks at the **Queen**.

Act Two

Scene One

Market Place

It is early evening.

The **Queen** *is on her knees, scavenging through a shallow wooden crate full of half-rotten vegetables.*

The **Queen Mother** *and* **Philomena** *sit side by side on a crate. Their job is to wipe and put the produce into a large shopping bag.*

Violet *is picking up fruit from the market floor and examining it.*

Queen Are you sure this is entirely legitimate Vi?

Violet I told yer', there's an' understandin'. Not a bad orange that.

Violet *passes the orange to the* **Queen Mother**, *who looks at it, doubtfully.*

Queen Mother It's covered in something horrid!

Philomena (*to* **Queen Mother**) Why d'you think an orange got such a thick skin, woman? To keep the germs from gettin' in. Give it a wipe.

The **Queen Mother** *wipes the orange, and gives it to* **Philomena** *who starts to peel it.*

Violet So, you'd wake up in the morning . . .

Queen Oh Vi! Not again . . .

Violet In your linen sheets.

Queen Yes.

Queen Mother Trimmed with Nottingham Lace.

Queen Yes, and my curtains would be opened, my tray would be brought in, and I'd drink my tea while somebody ran my bath. . . . Four half decent potatoes, jolly good.

Philomena Me arthritis playin' me up. Here Elizabeth, you peel it.

She gives the orange to the **Queen Mother**.

Queen Mother I don't know if I can . . .

Philomena Take the white gloves off woman! You hain't launchin' a ship!

The **Queen Mother** *takes her gloves off, and with difficulty starts to peel the orange.*

Violet Then you'd have your bath. How many radiators were there in the bathroom?

Queen You know how many, Vi.

Violet Four! . . . A Cox's Pippin. Only a bit bruised an' all. So it were lovely an' warm?

Queen Oh yes. Lovely and warm, and it smelt divine. Lavender oil.

Queen Mother We grew our own lavender at Sandringham.

Violet (*correcting*) The gardeners grew it. Go on, Liz.

Queen Then, if I had a public engagement, my hairdresser would come . . .

Violet And somebody would lay your clothes out . . . an' you wouldn't 'ave a bloke gerrin' in the way while you were dressin'.

Queen Oh no. Philip had his own rooms down the corridor. Rather a long way down the corridor.

The **Street Cleaner** *comes on and begins to sweep the market floor around the women.*

Violet 'E din't *bother* you much then?

Queen He hasn't *bothered* me for years. He made his own arrangements. Is this a parsnip?

Violet Yeah.

Queen Does one put a parsnip in one's stew?

Violet Yes, one does.

Queen Mother I've peeled an orange, Lilibet! Look! All by myself!

Queen Well done Mummy!

Philomena She want a brass band to play.

Violet (*to* **Queen Mother**) Stick your thumb in the middle and share it out then.

Queen I took an orange to Charles in prison, but they wouldn't let him have it.

Philomena The boy needs his Vitamin C.

Queen I could have injected it with drugs, apparently.

Queen Mother But you hadn't?

Queen Of course not, Mummy!

Street Cleaner 'Ow long you gonna be, only I've got me dinner waitin'.

Violet Ain't you the lucky one.

Queen Dreadfully sorry, we'll be out of your way soon. Carrots, Violet!

Violet Right, coupla decent onions an' we've gorrus stew.

Street Cleaner You should be ashamed o' yourselves.

He starts to move away.

Violet Shut your faxin' gob.

Street Cleaner Three minutes, then I'm tellin' the
Inspector. Grubbin' in the muck like dogs.

Violet Fax off! Yer only a faxin' brush pusher yerself!

Queen Violet, let's go.

Street Cleaner Three faxin' minutes. Dogs! (*He walks off.*)

Violet (*shouting*) Do you know oo you're calling a dog? The
Queen, and I, Violet Toby, that's who!

The **Street Cleaner** *has gone. The women are quiet.*

Violet (*to the* **Queen**) Why din't you stand up for yourself?

Queen He made me feel ashamed. (*Long pause.*)

Violet He made *me* feel ashamed. Think I'd be used to it by
now, wun't yer? I've never 'ad nowt. (*She wipes her eyes
angrily.*) That faxer's upset me now!

Queen Mother Would you like some of my orange, Violet?

The **Queen Mother** *gives* **Violet** *a segment of orange.*

Violet I've worked 'ard all my faxin' life, so did me 'usbands
'til the work went. I still ain't got a warm bathroom.

Queen Are these tomatoes too squidgy?

Violet No, they'll fry up.

Philomena You're poor cos you ain't educated, Violet. I
never known an educated person who was poor.

Violet I were clever at school! But me Mam needed the
money.

Queen So you went to work?

Violet I 'ad to. I gave me Mam me wages. She gev me
enough back for me bus fares an' a packet of nylons. Our

Mam 'ad seven kids an' three dogs, big uns. I only got married so I'd 'ave a bit of elbow room.

Diana *runs on. She is carrying a plastic bag.*

Diana I got the bones! The butcher was really sweet.

Violet *examines the bones.*

Violet 'Ow much you pay for these?

Diana Thirty-eight pence a pound.

Queen Thirty-eight pence! Did you tell the butcher they were for the dog?

Diana No, I haven't got a dog.

Violet Diana. If you're buyin' bones you always say they're for the dog, always. I *told* you.

Diana Sorry. I hate telling lies.

Violet Look. It ain't possible to be honest an' poor. Them days are gone.

Queen You must be more careful with your money Diana. William tells me you've acquired a video machine.

Diana It was terribly cheap.

Queen But hardly a necessity.

Diana It's necessary to me. I never go out, and if I can't watch *An Officer and a Gentleman* at least once a week I shall go mad! Thank God for Spiggy and his home deliveries.

Queen Diana, we have less than three minutes to find some onions.

Diana The butcher recognised me, said he used to be a fan.

Queen Mother The public used to love me, didn't they Lilibet? They truly loved me. 'God bless you, Ma'am', they'd shout.

Diana He was very sweet.

Violet Didn't stop him chargin' you too much for them bones.

Queen Mother The people were so cheerful during the Blitz.

Diana He asked me to autograph a sausage for his wife.

Queen A sausage! How very undignified. I hope you refused.

Diana No, I didn't know how to.

Violet Fancy writin' on a faxin' sausage!

Violet *laughs, the* **Queen** *joins in. They clutch each other.*

Philomena You'll have to come to assertiveness training wi' me, Violet.

Queen Violet, you're the most assertive person I know.

Violet I'm all right on the Estate, but I go to pieces in the town. I feel like I shun't be here.

Philomena Strange, hain't it. How a man's voice stop the breath in your body.

Violet I were a right doormat once. I used to read books 'til me second 'usband said it got on 'is nerves 'earing me turn the pages.

Philomena I was so happy the day the Lord took me husband. (*She looks up.*) I expect he's up there now, shoutin' and swearin' and fightin' with the angels.

Queen Philip's been in bed for four weeks. If I even suggest he gets up, he flies into a rage. He reduces me to jelly.

Violet I never did get to the end of *Tarka the Otter*. 'E broke me jaw, an' put me in the 'ospital for a week. I cun't eat, but it were a lovely break.

'What Makes the Husbands Leave Home' song.

Violet
    All he'd do at first would be to sit there staring
    With his face all red and his nostrils flaring
    Then without a by-your-leave he'd be banging and
        swearing
    And twenty minutes later I'd be well past caring
    They locked him up and moved me to a new estate
    But I knew that they'd release him on a certain date
    So I went along to meet him at the prison gate
    And he done me three days later with a broken plate

Wives
    Tell me testosterone, tell me male pheremone, please tell
        me Y chromosome
    What makes the husbands, what makes the husbands,
        what makes the husbands leave home

Leanne
    My little Malcolm would get stoned all day
    With his heavy metal records that he'd always play
    Though he wouldn't lift a finger in the normal way
    What his good points were I'd find it hard to say

Wives
    Tell me tamazepan, tell me nitrazepan, tell me phenol
        barbitone
    What makes the husbands, what makes the husbands,
        what makes the husbands leave home

Diana
    I'd be checking out the cardigans at Nicole Farhi
    He'd be bonding with a bushman from the Kalahari
    I'd bop with Phil and Elton, I'd smile and blush
    He'd shag that bag Camilla and get a Royal flush

Wives
    I had more than his fist when he staggered home pissed
    He was bad through and through I'm convinced

I was five years married and never been kissed
And I ain't seen a word of him since

Husbands
If you lose your Merthyr Tydfil you can try a Pontypridd
I had to go to Cardiff and I'm very glad I did
Rubbertitswith Aberystwyth, Carmarthen feel the noise
I'll wander up the Rhondda 'cos I'm back here with the
   boys

Wives
Tell me telepathy, holistic therapy, nam yoho renge kio om
What makes the husbands, what makes the husbands,
   what makes the husbands leave home

All
Tell me testosterone, tell me male pheremone, please tell
   me Y chromosome
What makes the husbands, what makes the husbands,
   what makes the husbands leave home

End of song.

Street Cleaner *enters.*

Street Cleaner Ain't you scavengers gone yet?

Violet No, we ain't, brush face.

Queen Terribly sorry.

Diana Are we in your way?

The **Street Cleaner** *recognises* **Diana**.

Street Cleaner Princess Diana! (*Pause.*) I din't vote for 'em.
I voted for lower taxes. Law an' order, keep the monarchy.
Don't you worry duck, you'll be Queen one day.

Diana That's very kind of you. What's your name?

Street Cleaner Derek Gringleton.

Diana I'm selling honours. It's two pounds for a Knighthood.

Diana *takes the brush from his hands, pushes him into a kneeling position, and taps both shoulders with the handle of the brush.*

Derek *gives* **Diana** *the money.*

Diana Arise, Sir Derek.

Street Cleaner Sir Derek! Thank you, Your Royal Highness.

Diana 'Night, 'night, Sir Derek!

Street Cleaner I shall have to get me name changed on the rent book. 'Sir Derek Gringleton of Eyres Monsell'. It's bound to impress 'em at the 'ousing office. Perhaps we'll get that transfer we've been after. (*Pause.*) What will the missus be now? 'Lady Maureen Gringleton'. She'll need to alter her weight watcher's card. Perhaps they'll show 'er a bit more respect. It's not her fault she's not reached her target. Ten stone is a lot to lose. It's her glands. I 'ope this is not going to change our lives too much, now we're aristocracy.

Scene Two

Community Centre

Trish *is directing an assertiveness training class. The* **Queen**, **Diana**, **Violet**, **Philomena**, *and* **Mrs Newman** *are sitting in a half-circle.*

Trish So, Diana, you're playing yourself. And who shall we have playing the butcher? How about you, Liz?

Queen No, I couldn't possibly.

Diana Oh go on. You used to be terribly good at Charades.

Queen But I've never spoken to a butcher, apart from Bomber Harris that is.

Trish Now come on, Liz. If we want to grow we have to take risks.

Violet (*to* **Queen**) On your feet! Now!

The **Queen** *gets to her feet instantly.*

Queen Violet, there is no need to be quite so brusque.

Violet I'm assertin' meself!

Trish Like all recent converts, Violet tends to be a bit over-enthusiastic at times.

Violet I've only 'ad three lessons, but I've already took a pair of shoes back to British Home Stores and got me money back.

Mrs Newman Good for you.

Violet I know, 'specially as I bought 'em from Woolies.

The women laugh.

Trish So, Diana, you come into the butcher's shop. Now, what's your objective?

Diana Objective?

Violet She wants to buy some bones.

Diana Yes, bones.

Trish But you *don't* want to autograph a sausage, do you?

Violet *and* **Mrs Newman** *laugh.*

Trish What's so funny?

Mrs Newman Sausage. It always makes me laugh.

Trish How very infantile, Mrs Newman. People who laugh at the word sausage usually had problems with their early toilet training.

Mrs Newman (*indignantly*) I didn't! I were outa nappies at ten month. If I bobbed myself after that I got hit on the head with the potato masher.

Trish (*to* **Diana**) You want to get out of the shop *with* your bones, but *without* being recognised, is that right, Diana?

Diana Sort of right.

Trish (*to* **Queen**) And what is *your* objective, butcher?

Queen My objective is to overcharge her for the bones, and get her to sign a sausage for my wife.

Trish You've grasped the concept. Excellent, Liz.

Queen Can I have a name? It may help me to find my character.

Trish Liz, it isn't important.

Queen Shall I be called Arthur?

Trish Liz, assert yourself. *State* that you are to be called Arthur.

Queen I am Arthur, the butcher. Arthur Wainwright.

Trish So, you busy yourself in the shop, Arthur. Chopping the meat, or whatever it is that butchers do. I'm a vegetarian, so it's a blank canvas to me . . .

The **Queen** *mimes butchering.*

Diana Some people came in after me. A man with a Scottish accent, and a woman who bought a frozen turkey.

Trish Violet, you play the Scotsman, Mrs Newman, you're the woman.

Philomena What about me?

Violet You can play the turkey. Get behind the counter. Cross your legs and stick an onion up your bum.

All the women apart from **Philomena** *and* **Trish** *laugh.*

Trish Violet! I'm directing this scenario. If you continue to be disruptive . . .

Violet What?

Trish *backs down.*

Trish (*to the group*) Can we start please? Walk into the butcher's shop, Diana. Scotsman, woman, Diana will give you your cue.

Diana *mimes, rather badly, opening a door.*

Queen Good afternoon, welcome to my shop. I am Arthur Wainwright. How may I help you?

Diana (*to* **Trish**) Actually, he was quite rude. He was cutting a sheep's head off, and he didn't even look up.

Trish OK, come in again. (*To* **Queen**.) Not quite so fulsome Liz, eh? Not the jolly butcher from the playing card.

Diana *mimes coming into the shop, the* **Queen** *mimes cutting a sheep's head off.* **Diana** *waits.*

Trish Liz, what are you doing?

Queen I'm cutting off a sheep's head, with an axe.

Trish Don't get carried away by the details. Remember your objective. You are an authority figure, you are Arthur Wainwright.

Queen I do know something about what it's like to be an authority figure, Trish. I *was* the Queen.

Trish But you were playing a symbolic role, Liz. Your life has been an *illusion* of authority fed by the projected fantasies of a credulous public. As Arthur Wainwright you have true authority. Embrace it.

Queen So, I don't cut off the sheep's head. . . ?

Trish (*irritably*) Can we start, please!

Diana *comes into the shop.*

Queen Good afternoon.

Diana (*to* **Trish**) He didn't say good afternoon.

Trish Oh for God's sake! Carry on.

Diana I'd like two pounds of bones please, Mr Wainwright.

Queen Bones? Are they for your dog?

Diana No, I haven't got a dog.

Queen Ah, then I shall charge you double the price.

Trish Good Liz, good. Diana, are you going to stand for that?

Diana That's terribly unfair, Mr Wainwright.

Queen I need to make a profit.

Diana (*to* **Trish**) The Scotsman came in now.

Violet *reels into the shop, drunkenly singing 'I Belong to Glasgow'.*

Trish Violet! Violet! Diana said he was a *Scot* not that he was a drunk.

Violet Well I've never known a jock that din't have a bottle in his pocket.

Queen (*to* **Diana**) So, are you taking these bones? I will charge you ninety-pence a pound.

Diana I suppose so.

Trish Assert yourself, Diana.

Diana (*to* **Queen**) No. I'll go somewhere else.

Violet (*Scots accent*) Tesco's lassie. Twenty-five pence a pound.

Diana Thank you.

Trish Second objective, Liz?

Queen I know who you are. You are Princess Diana.

Diana The woman comes in now.

Queen You're not leaving this shop until you've signed a sausage for my wife.

Mrs Newman (*laughing*) Sausage!

Philomena *goes and lies down on the counter. She folds her arms and crosses her legs.*

Trish Aren't you well, Philomena?

Philomena Don't talk to me, I'm the turkey.

Trish Diana. Are you going to sign that sausage?

Mrs Newman (*laughing*) Every time I hear it! Sorry.

Trish You're in a state of near hysteria. Pull yourself together, Mrs Newman.

Mrs Newman (*to* **Trish**) I can't help it. I feel daft. I don't know what to do. I don't see 'ow this is goin' to 'elp me.

Trish Trust me, Mrs Newman. I know what I'm doing.

Violet She's got qualifications in all this daft stuff, ain't you, Trish?

Mrs Newman I can't get me son to go to school. 'E lies in bed lookin' at comics.

Trish Assert yourself. Arthur Wainwright is your son. Stand up to him.

Mrs Newman Darryl.

Queen (*to* **Trish**) So I'm now Arthur and Darryl and Elizabeth Windsor?

Trish Yes. Carry on.

Queen (*to* **Diana**) What did you sign the sausage with?

Mrs Newman *laughs*.

Diana A black marker pen. 'To Beryl, Love Diana.'

Queen Love? To a woman you've never met? On a sausage. I think you *wanted* to sign that sausage.

Trish Diana. Did you or didn't you?

Diana I sort of did want to sign it, yes.

Violet Well. She were a star, weren't you Di? Must be hard bein' ordinary again.

Queen There are advantages to being ordinary. Diana refuses to acknowledge the fact.

Diana Name one advantage!

Queen That we no longer have to sit through a Royal Variety Performance. I fear you've become addicted to fame, Diana.

Diana Look, Arthur Wainwright, I married Charles because I loved him. I didn't 'specially want to be Queen.

Trish Good Diana. Stand up to him.

Mrs Newman Excuse me. I'm in an 'urry, can I 'ave a frozen turkey, and would you mind getting out of bed, please?

Queen Wait your turn, can't you see I'm serving another customer?

Diana I felt sorry for Charles. He was so damaged by his childhood, *Mr Wainwright*.

Queen Nonsense! He was a very happy little boy, *customer*.

Diana How would you know, *butcher*? You hardly saw him.

Queen Because, *bone buyer*, his Nanny told me.

Trish Excellent! Well done. Try again Mrs Newman.

Mrs Newman Sorry to bother you, Darryl. But I think you ought to get out of bed now pet, and go to school.

Queen Fax off, Mum!

Trish (*to* **Mrs Newman**) Don't *ask* him. *Tell* him!

Mrs Newman Get out of bed and go to school. If you wouldn't mind, there's a good lad.

Diana (*to* **Trish**) Do I take my bones and go?

Violet Yeh, give *us* a chance. I've said nowt yet. Gissus a Haggis lassie.

Queen (*to* **Violet**) You are drunk! Leave my shop immediately. (*To* **Diana**.) Take your bones and get out! (*To* **Mrs Newman**.) I refuse to get out of bed and go to that appalling school with the leaking roof and the empty library shelves! And while you're about it, give me ten pounds, collect your turkey, and go!

The women follow the **Queen***'s instructions.* **Diana** *runs out.* **Mrs Newman** *tries to pick up* **Philomena**. **Violet** *and* **Trish** *help, leaving the* **Queen** *alone in the room. The* **Queen** *asserts herself to her* **doctor***.*

Queen Dear Doctor, I know psychiatric beds are extremely scarce, and that it's easier to get into Eton, but I'm afraid I must insist that a bed be found for Philip. He's refusing drink, food, and soap. He needs proper professional care in an establishment with a garden and high walls. The Community does not care for him, and I am worn out from witnessing his misery. Find him a bed! Yours sincerely, Arthur Wainwright, Butcher.

Scene Three

The Queen's living room

Violet *helps* **Philip** *down the stairs.*

Philip Let me go!

Violet Come on now, me duck.

Philip I'm due to address a World Wildlife dinner in Vancouver at one.

Queen Your transport is on its way, darling.

Philip Who are you calling darling? Don't know you, do I?

Queen I'm your wife, Elizabeth.

Philip I'm married to the Queen.

Queen I used to *be* the Queen.

Philip Let me see the back of your head.

The **Queen** *turns her head.*

Philip Yes, recognise you now. Walked behind you long enough. Where's that helicopter?

Violet It's on its way, duck.

Philip (*touching* **Violet***'s face*) Is that you, my love? Is it Hélène?

Violet No. It's Violet Toby.

Philip I once knew a person called Violet Toby. A frightful, lower-class, opinionated woman. She lived on a council estate. She was a bad influence on the Queen.

Queen I'm sorry, Vi.

Violet S'oright, he don't know what 'es sayin'.

Queen (*to* **Philip**) Who is Hélène, darling?

Philip Who?

Violet (*kindly*) It's best not to ask, Liz.

Queen (*stroking* **Philip***'s hand*) He was such a beautiful young man. A Greek god. I adored him from the very first moment I saw him.

Philip The day the Queen's father died, I died with him.

Queen Philip, what do you mean?

Violet He's just rambling. My granddad went like this. They'll say owt.

Philip The King is dead, long live the Queen. Wasted my life.

Queen No! You've contributed (*Slight pause.*) a great deal.

Philip Spent my time touring light engineering factories on industrial estates.

Queen Not *all* the time. You've written books . . . *The Wit and Wisdom of the Duke of Edinburgh* . . .

Philip Where's the helicopter? Can't wait to get out of this place. On top of each other day and night. No space. No privacy. No function. Thought I was coming to a *country* estate!

Violet Where's that bleddy ambulance – I mean helicopter?

Philip Why was I punished? Was it my fault my sisters married Nazis?

Queen Philip, nobody is blaming you! (*To* **Violet**.) It was very awkward having one's brother-in-law in the Luftwaffe.

Philip My uniform correct? Buttons polished?

Queen You look immaculate, as always darling.

Mr Slobby *appears – a large doll-like figure, covered in spots. Only* **Philip** *sees him.*

Philip There's a thing in the room. (**Philip** *cowers.*) Is it Fergie?

Violet (*to* **Queen**) He's seein' things now. I'll go and find out where that ambulance 'as got to?

Violet *stands up and sees* **Mr Slobby**.

Violet Oh 'ello! You've called at a bad time. There's trouble in the house.

Queen Violet, do you know this person?

Violet Everybody knows him, Liz. He sort of stands for England now you've gone.

Philip Tell it to go away!

Queen Please leave, you are upsetting my husband.

Mr Slobby *takes his head off: it is* **Charles**.

Queen Charles!

Violet (*disappointed*) Oh, it's you. I were going to ask you for your autograph.

Queen Philip, it's Charles. Do you remember Charles?

Philip Of course I do. I love the boy.

Charles You do? Then why didn't you tell me?

Philip (*shouting*) I'm not an *American*, boy!

Charles Pa, please don't shout.

Violet I'll go and watch for that ambulance.

Charles Er . . . Mrs Toby you haven't seen me . . . should the police enquire.

Violet Right. *Have* I seen Mr y'know who?

Charles Yes.

Violet Right.

Violet *goes.*

Queen (*to* **Charles**) So you've come to say goodbye to Daddy before he is admitted to . . . *Vancouver* have you Charles?

Charles Vancouver?

Philip That helicopter's late! I was proud of you boy, the day you got your pilot's licence.

Charles You didn't show it at the time. You said any fool could learn to fly.

Philip Did I? Didn't mean it.

Charles I was terribly upset.

Philip Didn't show it.

Charles No, I was well trained. I learned to keep my hands behind my back and my emotions somewhere else.

Philip (*indicating Mr Slobby's costume*) This what you young people are wearing these days? Prefer you in a blazer.

Queen Charles, have you, as they call it on the estate, 'done a runner'?

Charles I was sentenced to four months, but those Group 4 security chaps were terribly kind. I couldn't go to prison, Mummy. I've been in prison all my life.

Queen I'm sorry I couldn't be there.

Charles You were never there.

Queen I didn't want to be out of the country so often, Charles. I was forced to travel to help the export drive. A futile waste, as it turned out.

Charles I met you at Waterloo Station once when you'd been away for months and you *shook my hand*. I was four years old.

Queen Yes, I remember. I should at least have taken off my glove.

Charles No. You should have kissed me! You and pa! It's strange Mummy but since leaving the joke shop one's had this terrific feeling of *release*. One's neither male nor female. One's just a *blob*. On my journey through the estate people smiled and waved to me with what looked like genuine affection even, dare I say it, respect.

Violet Ambulance is 'ere Liz!

Queen Philip, are you there, darling?

Philip Yes, but I should be in Vancouver.

Queen Philip. Kiss Charles, darling.

Sound of ambulance.

Philip Is that my helicopter? Will there be a red carpet?

Queen There'll be a red carpet.

Charles *and* **Philip** *embrace. The* **Queen** *joins them in the embrace, then picks up a small suitcase.* **Charles** *puts his Slobby head on and* **Philip** *is escorted to the ambulance.*

Scene Four

The Street – Hell Close

Philomena *and the* **Queen Mother** *totter on. The* **Queen Mother** *is holding her red purse.*

Philomena You should put your purse away woman. You want it snatched from your hand?

Queen Mother I think it's simply marvellous that we are given this gift of money every week.

Philomena It's a gift to you woman. But it hain't no gift to me. I paid me National Insurance every week for this pension.

Queen Mother I couldn't help but notice in the Post Office that you've got rather a lot of money in your handbag.

Philomena (*clutching her bag*) Me life savings in here.

Queen Mother Shouldn't they be in a bank?

Philomena No! Banks rob your money an' call it charges. Mrs Thatcher don't want me on this earth, eatin' an' drinkin' and keepin' warm.

Queen Mother But Mrs Thatcher has gone!

Philomena She'll come back! Just like the devil! I'm livin' on tea an' toast. They hain't sending me to the workhouse.

Queen Mother Tea and toast! But your larder is full of jars and tins and packets. It looks like Fortnum and Mason in there.

Philomena I tell you a secret Mrs Queen Mother. (*The women get closer to each other.*) All those jars an' packets an' tins are *empty*! (**Philomena** *laughs.*) What a trick eh! Nobody knows but you an' me. Fitzroy's been thinkin' I'm living like a Queen, but I hain't.

Leanne *and* **Charles** (*as* **Mr Slobby**) *come on.* **Mr Slobby** *has* **Clinton** *sitting on his shoulders.* **Leanne** *and* **Mr Slobby** *have their arms around each other.*

Leanne I finished that Henry V book you gev me last night. I thought it were good. He reminded me of you.

Mr Slobby *takes* **Clinton** *from his shoulders.* **Clinton** *cuddles into* **Mr Slobby**.

Leanne (*to* **Mr Slobby**) 'E luvs you, don't 'e? (*To* **Clinton**.) You love your new dad, don't you, Clinty? He does! He does!

Clinton Mr Slobby!

Leanne (*thrilled*) Did you hear him Charlie? His first words! 'Mr Slobby.' Did you hear him?

Mr Slobby *throws* **Clinton** *into the air and catches him three times.* **Clinton** *laughs.*

Leanne (*to* **Clinton**) You can 'ave a chocolate off the Christmas tree when you get 'ome. (*To* **Mr Slobby**.) 'Ave you got another book?

Mr Slobby *nods, and they walk off holding hands.*

Holyland Leanne. Mr Slobby. Been Christmas shopping?

Leanne Yeah. You caught that Charlie Windsor yet?

Holyland No, he'll have gone off to Wales with the rest of 'em. You can count the men left on this estate with the fingers of one hand now.

Mr Slobby *waves to* **Holyland**.

Mr Slobby, **Leanne** *and* **Clinton** *go off*.

Diana *and* **Fitzroy** *run on in sports gear. They have been for a three mile run. They stop to catch their breath. They rest their hands on their knees. Hang their heads and pant.*

Diana That was great. I really enjoyed that.

Fitzroy You're very fit. I had a job keeping up.

Diana I think it's really important to keep in shape. I mean once your muscle tone goes, you may as well be dead.

Holyland Very nice to see somebody round here taking some healthy exercise. Been far?

Fitzroy Three miles.

Holyland I came fifth in the Police Cross Country in 1979.

Diana Fifth! Well done!

Holyland I *was* quite pleased. (*He smiles*.)

Fitzroy *and* **Diana** *stand and look at each other. They smile.*

Fitzroy Lovely teeth.

Diana Fabulous smile.

Fitzroy Race you.

Diana *and* **Fitzroy** *race off*.

The **Queen** *and* **Violet Toby** *pass, carrying heavy shopping bags. Their arms stretched.*

Violet I can't wait to get these faxin' shoes off!

Holyland (*to* **Queen**) How's your husband, Ma'am? Is he making progress?

Queen Some, he no longer thinks he's in Vancouver, Inspector.

Holyland Good.

Queen He now thinks he's in Toronto.

Holyland So, progress of a geographical kind at least. I'm, er, having a bit of a soirée tomorrow night, Ma'am. Nothing elaborate, a few mince pies, the odd bit of Edam on a stick, I wondered if you'd care to join me?

Queen That is awfully kind of you.

Violet Ain't I invited?

Holyland It's singles only, Violet.

Violet Yeah, but nobody goes out with their 'usbands nowadays do they? Not if they want a laugh.

Queen I'm not sure of my plans yet, Inspector, may I let you know?

Holyland Certainly, Ma'am.

Holyland *walks off.*

The **Queen** *and* **Violet** *stagger along with their bags, giggling.*

Violet Are you gonna go?

Queen I might. While Philip's in Toronto.

Two **Lost Boys** *up in the tower.*

What you doin'?
Thinkin'. I want sommat.
What?
I wanna be 'ardest.
But *you* ain't 'ard.
I need money. I wanna. I wanna shooter.
That's 'ard.
'An bullets.
That's 'arder.

I wanna pull the trigger.
That's 'ardest.
Respect.
So?
Money.

Scene Five

The Queen's Living Room

The **Queen Mother** *and* **Philomena** *are distressed. They are being comforted by* **Diana**. **Holyland** *is attempting to question them.*

Holyland   Can you describe these lads, ladies?

Philomena   Devils, they devils!

Diana   Can't this wait, Inspector? You can see how distressed they are.

The **Queen** *and* **Violet** *enter with their shopping bags.*

Queen   What's wrong?

Diana   Granny and Mrs Toussaint have been robbed!

Queen   No!

Violet   That's disgusting!

Philomena   It was William's friends. I saw them.

Diana   No! I know they're a bit rough but they wouldn't steal from pensioners!

Queen (*to* **Diana**) Where *is* William? (*Referring to* **Philomena** *and the* **Queen Mother**.) Are they hurt?

Diana   No, just terribly shocked.

Queen   Diana! *Where* is William?

Diana   He's at school.

Violet No 'e ain't. I just seen 'im on the reccy.

Queen Mother William's friends took my red purse away, Violet.

Philomena They took me life away. I'm going to the workhouse.

Violet I'll bleddy crucify 'em. 'Anging's too good.

Holyland It shouldn't take long to clear it up now. (*To* **Philomena**.) Did you get a good look at them Mrs Toussaint?

Philomena No. They was wearing something over their faces.

Queen Mother They were William's friends.

Philomena Stockings.

Holyland (*disappointed*) So, you didn't actually *see* their faces?

Queen Mother No.

Philomena No. Devil boys.

Holyland Now that's a shame. It puts a new complexion on it.

Queen Are you doubting their words, Inspector?

Violet It was 'is scum-bag mates and everybody knows it!

Holyland But it's proving it in court, Violet.

Violet It wun't go to court if it were left to me.

Holyland You'd take the vigilante option would you Violet?

Violet I bleddy would! I'd get a few blokes together and I'd break their bleddy legs!

Queen (*cutting in*) I'd rather the police took care of it, Violet.

Violet The police! They're faxin' useless.

Queen No, they're a fine body of men.

Philomena They always stopping me boys in their cars.

Holyland (*angry*) You came running to us fast enough when your house got burgled, Violet!

Violet Yeah, an' a fat lot of good it did me an' all!

Spiggy *enters, struggling with* **William**.

William It weren't me! I weren't there!

Diana Let him go! What are you doing to him?

Spiggy (*to* **Diana**) He's got fifty quid on him. Ask him where he got it.

Diana Have you got fifty pounds on you darling?

William I found it.

William *shows the £50 note*.

Spiggy (*to* **William**) You're a liar. (*To* **Holyland**.) I was up me ladder, cleaning windows in Helmsley Road and I saw *him* and the *pond life* he calls his friends, sharing out a whole lot of money. Next thing I see is the old ladies crying in the street.

Queen Oh my God! William.

Violet *comforts the* **Queen**.

Violet (*to* **William**) Ain't your grandma got enough trouble!

Leanne *comes in*.

Leanne I've just 'eard, is it true?

Diana Darling, tell me that Mr Spiggy is mistaken, or even lying.

Queen (*to* **Diana**) How dare you infer that Mr Spiggy is a liar! He is a decent honourable man!

Diana I'm sorry, but I can't believe William would be involved in anything like this. . . .

Spiggy (*to* **William**) Tell Inspector Holyland who gave you that money.

William I told yer, I found it.

Violet 'E ain't gonna tell a copper is 'e? (*To* **Holyland**.) 'E'll tell us if you go away.

Queen (*to* **Violet**) No! We must deal with this *within* the law. (*To* **William**.) William, I don't believe you when you say you found this money.

William But *I* didn't know they'd stolen it!

Holyland So who gave it to you lad?

Diana William. It's a terrible thing to steal an old lady's purse.

Queen Mother It wasn't only our pensions, I think you should tell the Inspector how much you lost, my dear.

Philomena I had four thousand height hundred and thirty-three pound in me bag.

Queen Mother Her life savings, Inspector.

Stunned silence.

Violet Faxin' 'ell! An' I were going to get a collection up to replace it. No chance.

Holyland This is going to make the front page of the *Mercury* this is. (*Shouting.*) I want *names* from you, lad. Toot sweet!

William I *can't* tell you their names!

Queen You must, William.

Spiggy Somebody's got to put a stop to 'em.

Queen Mother William, they were very cruel.

Diana William, I've never hit you have I?

William No.

Diana No. But I shall, unless you tell me who these boys are.

William I can't grass on them. If I do I'm dead, Mummy!

Diana *shakes* **William**.

Diana And your great-granny and Mrs Toussaint could have been dead too!

Queen The shock could have killed them!

Holyland Names! Now!

William Stop it! You're doin' my 'ead in!

Violet I'll cave your bleddy 'ead in!

Leanne Wait 'til your Dad gets 'old of yer!

William I can't grass them up!

Violet All right, not to the coppers, but you can tell us. They can't get away with it.

Spiggy They're controlling this bleddy estate! We must be daft as brushes to have let this happen.

Violet They've even 'ad my bleddy washing off the line!

Leanne They nicked my pushchair, an' wrecked it, an' it's not even paid for.

Philomena We're too scared to leave the house after dark, hain't we, Elizabeth?

Queen The boys are out of control.

Spiggy Because people won't stand up and be counted. They'll see 'em wreckin' a bus shelter and they'll cross over the road without sayin' owt.

Holyland That's what makes our job so bloody impossible.

Violet Because nobody wants to grass! You have to stick to your own kind! It's one of our rules.

Holyland Even if your own kind is destroying you?

Spiggy An' one of the rules used to be that you don't nick off your own kind. What happened to that?

Diana William, please tell the Inspector for Mummy.

William I'm not grassin' nobody up. I didn't know, honest, Mrs Toussaint. (*He gives* **Philomena** *the £50 note.*)

Spiggy So what are we going to do?

Queen (*to* **Holyland**) Inspector I think it might be best if we sort this out between us. You have my word that we will not break the law.

Holyland Going to solve the crime wave are you? Well, when you've done it, perhaps you'll let the London, New York, and Moscow police chiefs know how it's done. I learned my nine times table under your portrait, Ma'am. When I got stuck I used to look up to you.

Spiggy An' we used to look up to you. But you've gev up on us, like everybody else.

Holyland I can't wait to get back behind a desk.

Holyland *goes.*

Queen (*to* **William**) Where will the boys be now?

Leanne They'll be in Karl's house.

William *doesn't answer.*

Violet I'll run down to the Prince of Wales and get some blokes out of the bar. They'll break their bleddy legs.

Diana I'll phone Fitz, shall I? Ask him to bring some friends.

Leanne My brother's dead hard.

Queen No, no more violence.

Spiggy We'll have to do it between us.

Philomena And with the Lord's help.

Diana We're adults and they're only children.

Queen We shouldn't be scared of them.

Philomena Children of the devil!

Violet Them lads were born bad.

Leanne I'm not comin'. They might take it out on Clinton.

Violet *I've* crossed the street to avoid 'em a few times. I've shut me eyes to things I shun't a done.

Spiggy I don't *relish* tackling them. Just me and a bunch of women.

Queen Mother I'll come with you, Lilibet.

Philomena I want to haxe them boys for me money.

Leanne They won't *give* it to yer!

Violet We'll have to take it off 'em, won't we.

William They'll never let you into the house, Granny.

Diana Then we'll stand outside and wait.

Queen And if we outnumber them . . . ask other people to join us.

Violet Yeah. They'll see we mean business then, won't they?

Spiggy They'll know we've had enough.

They go, leaving **William** *alone.*

William I didn't grass, but I'm already dead, socially. You belong in the hardest gang or you don't exist. I could start my own, but that would lead to tiresome clashes and challenges. I don't lack courage. My family revelled in dangerous sports. I've skied and sailed and ridden horses, but I've never, never, felt so alive as I did when being driven at ninety miles an hour in a stolen car with somebody at the wheel who didn't care whether he lived or died. There's nothing much to get out of bed for here. At least Karl makes things happen.

Scene Six

Hell Close – night

Violet *comes on, she is quite drunk.*

Violet Come on! Come on! We're goin' to my house for a drink!

The **Queen** *and* **Spiggy** *come on. They are followed by* **Diana**, **Leanne**, **Queen Mother** *and* **Philomena**. *All slightly tipsy.*

Queen No Violet, it's been a very tiring day, and I've had quite enough to drink.

Spiggy I'll see you to your door, Mrs Windsor.

Violet What's wrong with my 'ouse eh? You're insultin' me! You want to get off with Spiggy don't you!

Queen Don't be so absurd, Violet.

Spiggy Now you're insulting *me*, Mrs Windsor.

Queen Perhaps a quick drink.

Violet Come in! Come in! 'N' 'ave a drink!

Leanne He's the first bloke I've 'ad who's never laid a finger on me and made me cry.

Diana Oh he won't *hit* you Leanne, he'll just *bore* you to tears.

Violet This way! My house!

Queen Mother Shall we have a nightcap with Violet, my dear?

Philomena Yes, but honly for the shock we's had.

Violet (*shouting outside*) Come in an' celebrate!

Holyland *comes on.*

Holyland Violet! Keep the noise down will you?

Violet We've bin' celebratin' in the club.

Holyland Got all the money back did you?

Violet No.

Holyland Half?

Queen Mother No.

Holyland Quarter?

Philomena No, honly height hundred and twenty-three pounds.

Queen And a video camera, Inspector, which we confiscated and gave to Mrs Toussaint.

Philomena Waste a time 'cos I don't know how to use the damned ting . . . sorry Lord.

Holyland Doesn't seem much to celebrate to me.

Queen It's a start. Anyway Christmas is coming.

Violet (*shouting*) Wilf! Let me in! I've not got me key!

Holyland Violet, you're disturbing the peace!

Violet Wilf, open the door!

Violet *kicks at the door.*

Holyland I hope young Clinton is not in a 'Home Alone' situation, Leanne.

Leanne No, he's not! His new dad's babysitting.

Diana Wills is round there too. Mr Slobby is getting really domesticated.

Leanne I know, he's teaching me how to cook them lentil things.

Diana Poor you. That means you'll have to *eat* them as well.

Violet (*maudlin*) He's doin' it deliberate. 'E 'ates company. I should never have married the miserable bugger.

Queen Violet, it's late. Perhaps we should all go home.

Violet (*to* **Queen**) Stay there! He said 'e'd take me away from all this. He promised me radiators.

The **Queen Mother** *takes out a bottle of gin.*

Queen Mother Shall we have a nip to keep out the cold?

She passes the bottle to **Philomena**.

Philomena Violet, if I'd known me money was going to be stole, I would have *bought* you some radiators, girl.

Queen Mother And if I'd known you had over four thousand pounds I wouldn't have paid your bus fare on Friday!

Spiggy Is Wilf *in*, Violet?

Violet 'E's always in. 'E's probably snorin' in front of the telly. (*Shouting.*) Wilf! Open the bleddy door!

Philomena *starts to sing 'Oh Come All Ye Faithful' very quietly.*

The **Queen Mother** *joins in quietly. The bottle circulates.*

Spiggy What are you doing on Christmas Day, Mrs Windsor?

Queen I'm cooking a turkey for the family. I'm rather dreading it. How much do turkeys cost?

Spiggy You gotta be talkin' fifteen quid to feed your lot.

Queen Oh dear, as much as that?

Spiggy We'll have no Queen's Speech this year, will we?

Queen No, thank God.

Spiggy Just *The Bridge Over the River Kwai* again.

Leanne *and* **Diana** *join in the singing of 'O Come All Ye Faithful'.*

Violet The Queen's Speech were rubbish anyway, just a load of blather.

Spiggy Take no notice of her, she makes a nasty drunk does Violet. She'll be sorry in the morning

Violet I will be sorry. Sorry for myself. Nothing changes does it? You just go to bed an' wake up an' look out the winder an' it's still there.

Queen What's still there?

Spiggy All the rubbish. The wrecked cars, even the pavements are cracked. It's no wonder the kids don't play on 'em anymore.

Queen Now *you're* getting maudlin, Mr Spiggy. Shall I stand for the council and get the pavements mended?

Spiggy *and the* **Queen** *laugh.*

Violet You won't get in! We don't vote for your sort round here. It's your sort who's left us to faxin' rot!

Queen I think, Violet, that you're making false assumptions as to my political affiliations.

Violet Once a Tory, always a faxin' Tory!

Queen Violet, you're talking to somebody who was forced to meet with Margaret Thatcher once a week for thirteen years!

Violet There she goes again, dropping names!

Queen I much preferred the Labour men!

Spiggy Come on, come on, don't you two fall out. Not at Christmas time. Goodwill eh?

Mrs Newman *comes on. She is wearing reindeer horns on top of her headscarf. She looks ill.*

Queen I can't fall out with Violet, she's teaching me how to cook the turkey.

Diana It's simple isn't it? Don't you just thaw it out, and stuff the cavities?

Leanne (*laughing*) Yeah, you wanna try it some time!

Mrs Newman Why didn't you wait for me? I've just been sick in Leanne's bush!

Leanne I've only just had that pruned!

Mrs Newman I feel so bad. What am I going to do about myself?

Diana You could have electrolysis for a start.

Leanne I'm half-trained as a beauty therapist. I cun't get the money to do the other half.

Violet Wilf, open this door! I've got company waiting for a drink!

Mrs Newman No more for me, Violet. But I 'ad to 'ave a drink to celebrate Darryl being in Youth Custody.

Diana That's no cause for celebration, is it?

Mrs Newman It is for me. At least I know where he is. I shall sleep well tonight.

Queen Mother Join in, Lilibet. You used to love this carol. 'What's exhultation?' you would ask.

The **Queen** *joins in the singing.*

Violet *decides to conduct the singing. Everybody sings, 'O Come All Ye Faithful'. They enjoy it.*

Wilf Toby *comes on, pushing his battery in a pushchair.*

Violet Where the bleddy 'ell have you been?

Wilf I've been round the houses tryin' to flog this so's I can buy you some bathcubes.

Violet I don't want bathcubes. I want a warm bathroom. (*She sobs.*) I want radiators!

Wilf (*to company*) 'Ad a drink 'as she?

Spiggy One or two.

Wilf (*gently*) Come on, my duck. Don't cry. Come inside. (*To company.*) I done me best, but what can you do?

Spiggy We're all redundant, Wilf.

Wilf You get the money back?

Philomena No. We found some hidden in the house, behind a water pipe.

Queen Mother Mrs Toussaint very kindly took us to the working-men's club.

Philomena An' spent money on drink, Lord forgive me.

Violet (*screaming to* **Queen**) You 'ad my radiators! You 'ad four and I 'ad none, an' that ain't fair!

Wilf (*steering* **Violet**) Come in my duck, come in.

They go inside.

Philomena Well I'm going home to say me prayers.

Queen Mother (*to* **Queen**) Goodnight, Elizabeth. We had rather a lot more than *four* radiators didn't we?

Queen Considerably more.

Diana We had at least four hundred bathrooms, between us. (*To* **Philomena** *and* **Queen**.) We'll see you home. Coming Leanne?

Leanne Yeah. I'm looking forward to a bit of exultation.

Diana What's he buying you for Christmas?

Leanne A bedside lamp.

Diana Leanne! Will you drape it with a red silk scarf?

Leanne Why would I want to do that?

Diana I don't know, disguise your stretch marks.

Leanne I haven't *got* stretch marks.

Mrs Newman I have.

Leanne The lamp's for me to read by. If he wants owt else, he puts the light *out*.

Diana But keeps his socks on.

Leanne Yeah!

Diana *and* **Leanne** *go off laughing*.

Mrs Newman Wait for me. (*Starts to go but stops and turns to* **Queen**.) You can come back to my house if you like.

No response.

I've gotta home-made Christmas cake.

No response.

It's got six eggs in it.

Queen *shakes her head*.

Nobody ever comes to my house.

Mrs Newman *exits, in tears.*

The **Queen** *and* **Spiggy** *walk to the* **Queen***'s front door.*

Spiggy Well, I'll say goodnight.

Queen Yes. Goodnight.

Spiggy I'll miss the Queen's Speech.

Queen It was a speech. But I didn't ever *say* anything.

Spiggy Wasted opportunity then.

Queen I had no true power, Mr Spiggy.

Spiggy No, but you had influence. You could have made things happen.

Queen No more than you could.

Spiggy Me? I just go with the flow, we all do. We react to events.

Queen It would be rather exciting to make something happen, wouldn't it? Goodnight Mr Spiggy.

Spiggy 'Night.

Queen *goes into the house.*

Spiggy *exits singing 'O Come All Ye Faithful'.*

Scene Seven

The Queen's kitchen

The **Queen** *is unwrapping a Christmas present.* **Margaret** *is watching, smoking a cigarette.*

Queen This is very kind of you Bud, I'm afraid I haven't bought you anything.

Margaret Don't get too excited Lilibet, it's only a book.

The **Queen** *takes the book from the wrapping paper. It is a Delia Smith cookery book.*

Queen Bud, how marvellous! Delia Smith. What a godsend, thank you.

Margaret You say you haven't bought me anything?

Queen No Bud, I'm in a terrible mess. I've invited the family to a turkey dinner and I haven't a turkey.

Margaret Then buy one.

Queen There isn't enough in my purse to buy the *giblets*. Diana tells me that you occasionally lend money.

Margaret No, I *often* lend money. I provide financial services to the poor. And I'm extremely good at it.

Queen You couldn't lend me twenty-five pounds could you? For Christmas.

Margaret Of course, darling.

The **Queen** *hugs* **Margaret**.

Queen Thanks Bud. I'm truly grateful.

Margaret For what you are about to receive.

Queen Christmas is so expensive. I had no idea. Remember Sandringham. That huge tree in the hall. And on Boxing Day, one's ponies . . .

Margaret Oh, yes. One lived for one's ponies. One's animals were so . . . forgiving.

Queen If you could lend me the money I could just about get to Penguin's Palace . . .

Margaret I'm so enjoying my career.

Queen They close at seven.

Margaret It's so marvellous to be able to relieve the people's financial anxieties.

Queen Perhaps if I run.

Margaret I've come from behind your shadow at last.

Queen I'm very pleased for you. The money, Margot.

Margaret Lilibet, you did *forget* to invite me to Christmas lunch, did you?

Queen (*lying*) Of course, you're most welcome to come.

Margaret No, I'm never welcome, but I'll come all the same, Lilibet. If I lend you *thirty* pounds, will you buy me a Christmas present?

Queen There's something I can give you instead. I've no use for it any more.

The **Queen** *takes a small crown out of a bread bin and gives it to* **Margaret**.

Queen It's nothing much, it's only a small one.

Margaret No, it's lovely. It's exactly what I've always wanted.

Queen Please, the turkey, Margot.

Margaret Yes, twenty-five pounds . . .

She gives the **Queen** *the money.*

Margaret . . . almost, but not quite interest-free.

Margaret *puts the crown on her head.*

Scene Eight

The Community Centre

Wilf *pushes a pushchair, containing his battery and a tool box. He picks the battery up, places it exactly and begins to wire it.*

Fitzroy *comes in carrying the camcorder.*

Fitzroy I hope you know what you're doing.

Wilf I know exactly what I'm doin'. I were an electrician at the Gas Board for twenty-five years.

Fitzroy Yeah, but the technology's moved on, Wilf.

Wilf I've kept up. I read the journals in the library. Me work were me 'obby.

William *comes on carrying a satellite dish.*

Fitzroy Where d'you get that?

Wilf Don't ask.

William It's all right, it's from an outer suburb.

Wilf Giz it 'ere.

Wilf *takes charge of the dish.*

William Can I help?

Fitzroy Yeah, keep out of the way.

Wilf No, he can be my apprentice. You can do the sound. Pass me a Philips screwdriver. (*Pause.*) That reminds me, 'ows yer Grandad?

Fitzroy Well, don't blame me if nobody's heard. I'm not taking the responsibility.

William He's still in Toronto. Is this a Philips?

Wilf Yes. Good lad. See, what I'm doing is bouncing a signal to the satellite and making a link. I've got the transponder round the back.

William Where's the satellite?

Wilf Now that's the problem William, the bleddy thing keeps moving round the sky.

The **Queen Mother** *comes in.*

Queen Mother Will I be in the way here? The kitchen is full of smoke and steam and Clinton.

Wilf Mind the cables, we don't want you tripping.

Violet *enters with a tree.*

Violet Wilf, givvus hand

Wilf Where did you get that?

Violet The vicar donated it.

Wilf Does he know?

Violet Not yet.

Queen Mother I like to watch people at work.

Fitzroy (*genially*) Well, you've done it most of your life haven't you; watched people fetch and carry.

Queen Mother (*hurt*) I can do many things for myself now. Draw my own curtains, many things.

Violet Can you fix me chasers?

Wilf I haven't got enough sockets.

Violet Well use your bleddy battery.

Fitzroy (*to* **Queen Mother**) So how have you contributed to this event, Mrs Bowes-Lyon?

Queen Mother I've given my opinions to Mr Spiggy and he was kind enough to write them down.

Leanne *enters.*

Leanne I shall need a table, chair, and good lighting. I'm going for quite a glamorous look.

Violet (*indicating the Christmas tree*) Fitz. How's this?

Fitzroy Great Violet. But we don't want it sprouting out her head. (*To* **Leanne**.) Make-up over there.

Leanne *moves to make-up area.*

Spiggy *comes on, reading from a piece of paper, he has a pen in his hand.*

Spiggy I need somewhere quiet to write.

Wilf How's it going, Spiggy?

Spiggy I'm not happy with it. You don't realise how important bleddy words are until you come to write the buggers down. I've been up all night.

Wilf You shun'ta volunteered.

Spiggy I know. I've rewritten the bleddy thing I don't know how many times.

William Put it in one sentence. That's what they taught us at Ludgrove.

Wilf (*to* **Spiggy**) You've never 'ad a problem wi' words before. I've seen you clear the bar in the club before now going on about what's wrong wi' the country.

Spiggy It's easy to *talk* though, in't it. It was findin' out what to *do* about it that's 'ard.

William It would do my head in.

Violet This all right, Fitz?

Fitzroy Magic, Vi.

Violet I've got some balls.

The **Queen** *enters in her finery, wiping her frock.*

Queen Did you do the rewrites, Mr Spiggy?

Spiggy *hands the paper to the* **Queen**. *She reads it.*

Spiggy I'm still not happy with it.

Queen (*to* **Violet**, *indicating* **Queen**'s *dress*) Giblet gravy all down it.

Violet Don't worry about me duck. I'll sponge you down.

Leanne I've got some kitchen roll here.

Violet *takes kitchen roll and sponges* **Queen** *down.*

Queen (*to* **Spiggy**) Why have you crossed out the bit about unemployment?

Violet *exits with dirty kitchen roll.*

Spiggy Because people are sick of hearing about it. They don't tek it in any more.

Leanne Come on, Mrs Windsor, I want to get going on your base.

Queen Then rephrase it!

Leanne I'm going to go for pinks, really bring up your features.

Wilf It were better when people were working. You can't leave that bit out, Spiggy.

Fitzroy The recession's been good to me.

Spiggy Well that's not going in, or you can find yourself another writer.

Spiggy *sits down and starts to scribble.*

Queen These are my notes, perhaps you can incorporate them into the text. You'll find a lot in there about unemployment. Well, look what happened to Philip, and there's a huge question mark over Wills.

Leanne Have you always had dry skin?

The Christmas tree lights come on.

William It works Wilf!

Wilf Of course it bleddy works!

Violet *enters, carrying a home-made crown, decorated in jelly-tots as a substitute for jewels.*

Violet That bleddy Clinton ate half the jelly-tots. How'ma s'posed to finish decorating this bleddy crown?

William I've got some Smarties.

Violet *No*, I've got a *vision*, William, and it don't say Smarties. (*To* **Leanne** *irritably*.) Can you leave her alone for a sec so I can try it for size?

The **Queen** *hands* **Spiggy** *a piece of paper*.

Leanne Violet, I've got a lot to do. I'm doing a glamorous look.

Spiggy We've already *got* a Constitution!

Queen Not a people's Constitution. Nothing is written down.

Violet I thought a constitution were a healthy walk.

Wilf Shurrup, Violet, you're showin' your ignorance.

Violet Never mind the Constitution, what about the Community Centre funding?

Queen Mother I know about make-up, I met Helena Rubinstein once.

Leanne I stopped votin' when the Poll Tax come in. Just pass me what I say.

Violet *tries the crown on the* **Queen**'s *head*.

Violet Too big. I 'ope you've kept that bit in about the damp 'ouses.

Queen Spiggy? Is the damp bit still in?

Spiggy It's in.

Leanne Have you got the nurseries in? Clinton'll need one soon.

William Me and the lads want something to do.

Fitzroy And I want my Mum to be safe.

Queen Mother There was a nursery on each street corner during the war. The King and I visited several. Have you included the crime problem?

Spiggy Of course I 'ave! Nobody talk to me now. I've got to concentrate.

Leanne And nobody talk to the Queen. (*To* **Queen Mother**.) Rimmel base, 'Biscuit Beige'.

Fitzroy Leave it there, I want a wide shot.

Queen You seem to be calling for a revolution in the third paragraph, Mr Spiggy.

Leanne Shurrup, and suck your cheeks in.

Violet I wun't mind a revolution, least it'd be a change.

Spiggy This is a cry for help. How does that sound?

Queen Overwrought, Mr Spiggy.

Spiggy A change is all we're askin' for, isn't it?

Wilf Violet, if your stiletto goes through that cable, you'll go up like Joan of Ark.

Violet There's millions like us, what they going to do with us eh?

Spiggy We want somebody to remember we're here, that's all.

Diana *makes her entrance.*

Fitzroy Princess!

Diana I didn't know what to wear, I'm not too overdressed?

Fitzroy Is a star too bright?

Violet You used to talk to me like that once, didn't you, Wilf?

Wilf Don't distract me Violet, not while I'm working, pass me the wire cutters, lad.

William I'm apprenticed to Wilf, Mummy. I might be an electrician.

Diana Oh I think you can do better than be an electrician Wills.

Violet What's wrong wi' being an electrician? If it weren't for Wilf this wun't be 'appenin'.

Diana I'm sorry, Wilf.

Queen I must have a table.

Wilf My family built your family's palaces.

Spiggy We made the clothes you wore.

Queen I simply can't go on unless we can agree on what I'm going to say.

Leanne Pass me 'Romeo Rage'.

Violet Make it up as you go along!

Diana All you have to do is tell the truth. Violet, can you see my panty line?

Violet If you want the truth, yes.

Queen Could someone please get me a table.

Diana Can we have a rehearsal? I'd like to get it right.

Fitzroy (*to* **Diana**) I can't wait to get you out of here.

Diana I can't wait to go. I'm sorry, but that's the truth.

William (*to* **Fitzroy**) I warn you, Fitzroy, I shall be the stepson from hell.

Wilf William, get up there and adjust the dish a couple of inches to the left lad, bleddy satellite keeps moving round the sky. We haven't got much time.

Queen Mother Is what we're doing illegal, Lilibet?

Queen It's more an act of Civil Disobedience, Mummy. Don't worry about it.

Queen Mother But you were never disobedient.

Queen Please don't remind me, Mummy, you're making me nervous.

Violet *puts the crown on the* **Queen**'*s head.*

Violet How's that feel, duck?

Queen Fine, just fine.

Wilf Twenty seconds!

Queen What!

Leanne Open your mouth and stretch your lips.

Wilf It's passin' over, now!

Queen But we haven't finished the content! We haven't agreed what to say.

Spiggy What's she wearing a crown for, she's not the bloody Queen.

Violet You touch that crown I'll kill you, I spent three days on that.

Spiggy I thought that was the whole point.

Diana We haven't had a rehearsal.

William Good luck, Mummy.

Wilf Fitz, ten seconds.

Fitzroy Ten, nine . . .

Leanne Lick your front teeth.

Fitzroy . . . eight . . .

Spiggy Just tell them what you've learnt.

Fitzroy . . . seven, six . . .

Queen And I still haven't got my table.

Diana Where am I standing Fitz?

Fitzroy . . . five . . .

Wilf We want work.

Fitzroy . . . four . . .

Wills Summat to do.

Fitzroy . . . three . . .

Violet Change!

Fitzroy . . . two . . .

Spiggy Don't let us down.

Fitzroy . . . one. Quiet.

Diana Please don't adjust your sets. This programme is now being shown on all four TV channels, and is being brought to you by the newly formed Hell Close Residents' Committee. One of our residents, Mrs Elizabeth Windsor, my mother-in-law, would like to talk to you.

Queen Hello. I would like to talk to you, very briefly, about my recent experiences. I have been appalled to discover that my friends and neighbours have been forgotten, their talents and skills have been ignored. Too many of them feel that their lives have been wasted. The young in particular have turned to crime as a means of procuring both money and excitement. This is a cry for help from a small group of people who have had enough. We feel a deep anger about the manner in which this country has been run, and warn the new government that there must be change. My question is, what are you going to do about the forgotten people

'Life in Hellebore Close' song.

Queen
   Life in Hellebore Close
   All seemed terribly gross
   Spirits simply just dived

Funds simply never arrived
One felt glum and morose

All

What welfare provides when a country divides
Wouldn't serve for a family of elves
The policy seems to be damn the deprived
They can bloody well fend for themselves
There's no panacea; that is only too clear
And moaning's a waste of your breath
The chances are slim and the prospects are dim
And we're bloody well frightened to death

All

Living on four pounds a day
Is depressing and dreary and grey
Living on nothing at all
There's really no farther to fall

Queen

Hope in Hellebore Close
Nothing too grandiose
Rome wasn't built in a day
But at least we're having our say
That's what matters the most

All

So tell all your chums to get off their bums
And alter this state of affairs
Your future depends upon you and your friends
When nobody else bloody cares
When you're cold and you're tired and the meter's expired
And the giro's not due for a week
Just get off your arse and show us some class
Or else we'll be right up the creek

All

Living without any dreams is even more dread than it
   seems
But you know that your spirit won't die
If you get up and give it a try

So fax all the mockers who laugh at your efforts
The wankers who offer disdain
And at least you can say that you did it your way
With a hand a heart and a brain
Living on four pounds a day is depressing and dreary and
   grey
Living in permanent thrall is not really living at all

Queen

Living is why we're all here, and we're ready to start, it
   appears
So citizens give us a clue; what are we going to do?

All

What are we going to do?

End of song.

End of play.

ROYAL COURT WRITERS

The Royal Court Writers series was launched in 1981 to celebrate 25 years of the English Stage Company and 21 years since the publication of the first Methuen Modern Play. Published to coincide with each production, the series fulfils the dual role of programme and playscript.

The Royal Court Writers series include work by

Karim Alrawi
Thomas Babe
Neil Bartlett
Aphra Behn
Howard Brenton
Jim Cartwright
Anton Chekhov
Caryl Churchill
Sarah Daniels
George Farquhar
John Guare
Iain Heggie
Robert Holman
Ron Hutchinson

Terry Johnson
Manfred Karge
Charlotte Keatley
Paul Kember
Hanif Kureishi
Stephen Lowe
David Mamet
Mariane Mayer
G. F. Newman
Wallace Shawn
Sue Townsend
Timberlake Wertenbaker
Snoo Wilson